THE SAGES

THE SAGES

WARREN BUFFETT,
GEORGE SOROS,
PAUL VOLCKER,
AND THE
MAELSTROM *OF* MARKETS

Charles R. Morris

PublicAffairs
New York

Book Design by Timm Bryson
Set in 11 point Eldorado by the Perseus Books Group

Library of Congress Cataloging-in-Publication Data
Morris, Charles R.
  The sages : Warren Buffett, George Soros, Paul Volcker, and the
maelstrom of markets / Charles R. Morris. —1st ed.
     p. cm.
  Includes bibliographical references and index.
  ISBN 978-1-58648-752-2 (hardcover)
  1. Finance. 2. Investments. 3. Soros, George—Political and social
views. 4. Buffett, Warren—Political and social views. 5. Volcker, Paul
A. —Political and social views. I. Title.
  HG4521.M8447 2009
  332.092'273—dc22

                          2009010292

First Edition
10 9 8 7 6 5 4 3 2 1

CONTENTS

INTRODUCTION

America and the world are trapped in the deepest, longest recession in postwar history. That by itself is good reason to reflect on the careers of Warren Buffet, George Soros, and Paul Volcker. Buffett and Soros are among history's most successful investors, with a record of making money in good times and bad. Volcker is a regulator, one of the greatest of American civil servants, whose entire career has been defined by crises. And all three saw this one coming long ago.

That last fact is worth dwelling on. The *Wall Street Journal* ranked the nation's leading economic forecasters on the accuracy of their 2008 economic forecasts, using two key data points: 2007–2008 fourth-quarter to fourth-quarter real GDP growth, and 2008's ending unemployment rate.[1] There are fifty-one economists in the sample. The actual fourth-quarter to fourth-quarter real GDP change was -0.8 percent. Only Goldman Sachs's Jan Hatzius, who forecasted -0.4 percent—which, given the margin of error in the data, counts as a direct hit—had the right sign of the change. All the others expected positive real growth, with a mean estimate of 2 percent, and the top estimate a giddy 5 percent. On unemployment, all of the forecasters expected a much better outcome than the actual 6.9 percent. The closest any of them came to the real number was 6.2 percent, while the mean forecast was a rosy 5.2 percent, and the cheeriest, 4.3 percent.

Of the 102 separate forecasts, then, for both unemployment and GDP, 101 of them are wrong *in the same direction*. Note that the forecasts were made in late 2007 or early 2008, when the credit crunch had been dominating headlines for months, and the government was taking extraordinary measures to blunt its effects. And these are not casual forecasts. Every economist represents a major bank or forecasting service that competes for customers in part by the excellence of its research and the accuracy of its forecasts, and all have made large investments in forecasting models and economic data bases. But as a group, they didn't understand what was going on, or have even an inkling of its global effects.

These three greybeards, however—Volcker is eighty-one; Buffett and Soros are both seventy-eight—did understand, and said so. Soros started warning about the gathering "superbubble" in the late 1990s. Buffett was sounding the alarm about the excesses of financial engineering just a few years later. Volcker's worries are long-standing, but he did not publicize them while his successor as Federal Reserve chairman, Alan Greenspan, was still in office.

On the surface, they are very different men. Buffett and Soros have almost diametrically opposed investment styles. Buffett is the classic hyperanalytic value-seeker. He does deep research, buys relatively infrequently, and typically holds his positions for many years. Soros is the global predator, with feline sensitivity to quivers of disharmony in the economic flux. He moves in and out of positions quickly and omnivorously—commodities, currencies, stocks, bonds, wherever there is opportunity.

Volcker has never been a professional investor, but he deserves primary credit for the signal macroeconomic achievement of the past thirty years—slaying the inflation monster that was engulfing the American economy at the end of the 1970s. The stable global economic growth of the 1980s and 1990s was grounded on Volcker's conquest of inflation.

But their commonalities transcend the obvious differences. All three embody what the Romans called "virtue"—steadfastness, consistency, devotion to principle. J. P. Morgan called it "character." Principled consistency is not the same as blind adherence to dogma; it implies, rather, weighing and judgment and common sense. For Buffett and Soros, it is evidenced by their disciplined approaches to investing, their readiness to admit mistakes, their imperviousness to febrile enthusiasms. For Volcker, it is the granitic integrity that has made him the first person to call when authorities need an unflinching view on a possible scandal.

Both Buffett's and Volcker's prestige is such that their mere appearance on a platform with then president-elect Barack Obama, presenting his economic recovery plans, caused a jaded world to breathe a sigh of relief. Soros was also an early Obama supporter and behind-the-scenes adviser.

During their active careers, all three have seen the United States twice reign as global hyperpower, and twice fall from grace amid international overreaching and economic mismanagement.

The Great Inflation of 1965–1980 ended the era of America's near-total dominance of the post–World War II world. For the first time since the nineteenth century, America became a debtor nation, facing sharp competitive pressure from a revitalized Japan and Germany.

Volcker's victory over inflation vaulted America back into something like its old dominance, riding the crest of a broadly gauged transformation in business and communications technology, until the implosion of the great asset bubble of 1995–2005. The vast wealth transfers to China, India, and the resurgent petro-states during the bubble years have left the country wallowing in the deepest debt pit in history.

Significantly, each crisis followed a decade of near-unanimity among professionals on policy rules for managing the national economy. The "Keynesian consensus" was the unassailable doctrine in the run-up to the Great Inflation, much as the theories of the Chicago School "New Classicals" pumped up the great asset bubble.

Living through such violent reversals—and in Buffett's and Soros's case, profiting mightily from them—reinforced all three's deep skepticism of nostrums and academic certitudes. They are respectful of markets, but they know markets can take a long time to get things right. Disparate as Buffett's and Soros's investment styles appear, their core assumption is that markets are frequently wrong. Buffett buys, or invests in, valuable companies, and has almost no interest in the fluctuations of their stock prices. Soros sniffs out incipient bubbles and rides them, confident he can get out before they pop. Volcker, of course, has spent much of his life dealing with the aftermath of markets gone wrong—the breakdown of the gold standard, runaway inflation, the petrodollar bust, S&Ls, and now, as an Obama adviser, the great asset implosion.

In particular, they understand that financial markets relate to the idealized "Market" of theory as the shadows in Plato's cave do to reality. Financial markets are dominated by people investing other people's money, often in contexts where destructive behavior generates great fortunes.

Consider the ironies of the current economic cycle. Finance gurus, led by Alan Greenspan, convinced of the universal correctness of market outcomes, presided over a virtual withdrawal of financial regulatory oversight. Now, hardly a decade later, the entire banking sector is on its way to being nationalized, along with insurance companies, automobile companies, and possibly much more. CEOs are beating a path to Washington to plead for money and favor. Government economic power is steadily increasing, even as its debt spirals up and the dollar quivers on the edge of the abyss.

For true believers in free-market ideology, it is the worst of all possible worlds—and they brought it on themselves. Greenspan practically wept at the congressional hearing when he conceded that he had never imagined that market professionals could be so reckless and so wrong. And as the *Journal*'s forecasting tabulations suggest, as late as last year, mainstream economists still did not understand what was going on.

That recent history is the best reason for studying Buffett, Soros, and Volcker. The great inflationary episode of the 1970s exposed the deficiencies of a too-eager espousal of Keynesianism. The current crisis is a painful lesson in the dangers of a blind adherence to market dogmatism. The real world of markets and governments is one where fallible humans act on dimly perceived trends—or, in Soros's words, in a state of "radical uncertainty"—and frequently get it disastrously wrong. The careers of these three are stories of success under conditions of uncertainty.

This book comprises three extended biographical essays, one on each of the main protagonists, plus a concluding essay pulling together their histories and insights in light of the current crisis. The biographical essays make no pretense to full-blown biography; rather, they are offered as compact narratives of the "Sages'" careers as market players and influencers, with enough personal information to identify the predispositions they brought to those roles.

I got to know both Soros and Volcker during previous writing projects, and they were fully cooperative with this one. I caught Buffett at a time when he had declared a temporary interview blackout, but there is a vast amount of material—both by and about him—which was more than enough for my purposes. What I most enjoyed from an extended period learning about the three Sages and delving into their histories was that it confirmed that even today, in an age ruled by dogmatisms as rigid as those of medieval Spain, common sense, good judgment, mature experience, and humility in the face of what one does not know is still a path to great success.

SOROS

*G*eorge Soros, by any measure, is one of the half dozen or so of the world's most successful investors. For the thirty years from 1969 through 2000, when he retired from active fund management, Soros's Quantum Fund returned investors an average of 31 percent a year. Ten thousand dollars invested with Soros in 1969 would have ballooned to $43 million by 2000, a good three decades' work by any standard.

Soros is one of the diaspora of brilliant Hungarian Jews that has enriched the West since the rise of Nazism and Soviet Communism. His company includes the great mathematician and computer pioneer John von Neumann; the atomic scientists Edward Teller and Leo Szilard; cultural figures like the novelist Arthur Koestler (*Darkness at Noon*) and the film director Michael Curtiz (*Casablanca*); and Soros's younger contemporary, former Intel CEO Andrew Grove.

Born in Budapest in 1930, Soros grew up in a cultured but not wealthy family. His father, Tivadar, was an attorney who, as an Austro-Hungarian officer in World War II, was captured by the Russians and endured a long stint in a POW camp before engineering a group escape and a circuitous flight back to Hungary. Although he lacked ambition and was a bit of an operator, Tivadar was greatly admired by young George. His skills in flimflam, indeed, may have been ideal for surviving the Nazi occupation. Some 400,000 Jews were "deported" from Hungary by the Nazis, but Tivadar brought his family—his wife, Elizabeth, and his two sons, George and Paul—safely through the war by dint of bribes, false identities, and multiple hiding places. For fourteen-year-old George, the experience was thrilling—like *Raiders of the Lost Ark,* he later recalled. Conceivably, his youthful experience running risks in the face of a menace like the Nazis contributed to his legendary cool in financial dealings.[1]

During the unsettled interregnum between the Nazi withdrawal and the Soviet takeover of Hungary, George at seventeen decided to take his chances in London. His father covered his travel, and he had an additional small sum from a relative. He supported himself with odd jobs—swimming pool attendant, waiter, painter, even farmhand—while reading voraciously and waiting for admission to the London School of Economics. His reading interests centered on philosophy and about 1951, he discovered, and was deeply impressed by, Karl Popper's *The Open Society and Its Enemies.* Soros later befriended Popper and has regarded him as his philosophical lodestone ever since.

Popper was primarily a philosopher of science, analyzing issues like the meaning and truth of statements of physics. His *Open Society,* published in 1945, was a devastating critique of the methods of social sciences, with a special focus on how social science had been dragooned into the service of totalitarianism. Popper's special *bêtes noires* were Plato, Hegel, and Marx, all of whom imagined some form of inexorably unfolding historical progression toward (or in Plato's case, back to) an ideal society. In Popper's view, such constructs were not only nonsensical, but stifled free inquiry and fostered tyranny. The proposed antidote was his famous requirement of falsifiability as a test of meaningfulness. Since the sweeping claims of philosophy, religion, or politics were generally unfalsifiable, he contended, they lacked meaningful content.

Popper believed that while there was such a thing as objective "truth," human knowledge was always provisional. No matter how useful or long-standing, any falsifiable belief was always at the mercy of some new critical experiment. The best that humans could hope for was to advance the state of knowledge by the conscious, critical application of scientific method, producing ever-revised approximations to the truth.[2]

Surprisingly, given his taste for philosophy, and his intelligence and wide reading, Soros was only an indifferent student, and by his own report was poor at math. Although he had hoped to become a philosophy teacher, his grades were too low to land a teaching assistantship. After graduation, Soros finally caught on as a trainee at a London securities firm in 1953 and became an arbitrage trader—exploiting temporary price misalignments among similar securities. In 1956, frustrated at the stodginess of London's "City" firms, he emigrated to New York.

His timing was perfect. Europe was in full recovery mode, the original six-nation Common Market was moving from dream to reality, and big companies, especially in Germany, were rapidly making up commercial ground lost during the war. Although only in his late twenties, Soros was a natural cosmopolite, multilingual, and with a much better grasp of European investment opportunities than most American brokers. By 1967, he was research director of a substantial firm with a big international trading book and increasingly thinking of managing portfolios. His firm encouraged him, and, after a trial with a model portfolio, he created the Eagle Fund, a mutual fund, with $3 million of initial capital. It was very successful, and in 1969, the firm created the Double Eagle Fund with $4 million in capital. This was a hedge fund, with few of the limitations that constrained mutual fund managers, and Soros was on his way.

Despite his burgeoning financial career, Soros never relinquished his dream of succeeding as a philosopher. As it turned out, for the next quarter century, finance and economics were dominated by ruling ideologies that looked to Soros much like the political paradigms that Popper had attacked in *Open Society*. With a native skepticism sharpened by his Popperist intellectual apparatus, Soros evolved an investment strategy akin to that of an atheist coolly fleecing the natives in a land of religious idiots.

THE SHIFTING RELIGIONS OF ECONOMICS

The Kennedy administration marked the first broad ascension of academic economists to dominant influence in economic policy making. (The great influence of John Maynard Keynes in establishing the postwar monetary settlements was something of a special case.) At least a half-dozen star economists, all "neo-Keynesians," four of them from Harvard, had prominent seats in Kennedy's policy discussions.* The key campaign promise was to "get the country moving again," or to accelerate economic growth. Kennedy's own grasp of economics was fragile, so he looked to the economists to make it happen.

---

* The most influential were: Walter Heller from the University of Minnesota, James Tobin from Yale, and Kermit Gordon from Harvard, all of whom sat on the Council of Economic Advisers (Heller was chair); the remaining three also came from Harvard: David Bell, budget director; Seymour Harris, special adviser to the Treasury; and John Kenneth Galbraith, ambassador to India and all-around gadfly.

The experiment seemed to be an amazing success. *Time* magazine picked Keynes for its 1965 "Man of the Year" cover, and its lead story hailed the "new economics." Kennedy's economists, it gushed, "skillfully applied Keynes's ideas—together with a number of their own invention—to lift the nation through the fifth, and best, consecutive year of the most sizable, prolonged, and widely distributed prosperity in history."[3] It was an illusion, of course, as was demonstrated by the precipitate unraveling of the neo-Keynesian consensus during the inflationary debacle of the 1970s.

The intellectual vacuum left by the fall of Keynesianism was immediately filled by the monetarist free-market liberalism taught by Milton Friedman and his intellectual heirs at the University of Chicago. The interventionist bias of the Keynesians, they argued, merely interfered with the natural tendency of markets to reach optimum outcomes on their own. Their prescription was to reduce or eliminate market regulation and taxes on capital, restrict the size of government, and confine its financial role to providing steady, formula-based monetary growth.

Much as in 1965, the advent of the new orthodoxy coincided with a sharp economic revival—the 1980s Reagan recovery—which the monetarists took as full confirmation of their theories. But dreams of a new golden age of markets dissolved in the worldwide credit crunch of the 2000s. Free-market ideology, it turns out, was just cover for the extraction of great fortunes by an avaricious new class of financial operators running Ponzi games in housing and other highly leveraged debt. The wreckage of institutions and assets will take years to repair.

At bottom, the difference between neo-Keynesians and the monetarists is small. They are both built on highly mathematized notions of the economy, and the assumption that the natural state of a market economy is to be in equilibrium. Graduate students in economics, regardless of their department's ideological flavor, spend a great deal of time proving the existence and uniqueness of specific equilibria. (The neo-Keynesians' emphasis on mathematical models was a significant departure from Keynes's own emphasis on non-quantifiable factors like the "animal spirits" of investors.)

The neo-Keynesians were more ready than monetarists to assume that rigidities in the real economy—from privilege, unionism, illegal combinations—would often prevent the achievement of high-efficiency equilibria. The long, weary years of the Depression were the living example of an economy stuck far below its true potential. But they believed they could reliably nudge an economy to a more desirable state by a well-aimed kick in the form of a tax cut or a spending increase. As Walter Heller, possibly the most influential member of Kennedy's economic team, put it, economic management had become a science of "flexibility and fine-tuning."[4]

Monetarism was really a theory of government decked out as a theory of money.* Friedman's research in economic history con-

---

* A note on nomenclature: The congeries of theories that mostly originated at the University of Chicago, and which generally assume that market prices are almost always the most accurate guide to real values, now include besides "monetarism," variants such as "rational expectationism," "efficient markets hypothesis" (EMH), "real business cycle" (RBC), and others, collectively known as the "New Classicals." "Neo-Keynesian" is the mathematized version of Keynesianism that reigned in the 1950s and 1960s. The "New Keynesians" are present-day economists like Paul Krugman, who have tried to correct the deficiencies of neo-Keynesianism and incorporate some of the insights of the "New Classicals." When writing of the period from the 1960s through the 1990s, I will refer to the two camps as the "neo-Keynesians" and the "monetarists," as they were generally known at the time. Referring to the present day, I will use the "New Keynesians" and the "New Classicals." Finally, I will use "Keynesian" and "Chicago School" to contrast the two broad traditions, irrespective of period.

vinced him that inflation was "always and everywhere a monetary phenomenon"—if the supply of money rises faster than real economic activity, prices will rise. Further, he was convinced that every economy had a natural rate of employment, defined by its technology and the skills of its work force. Attempts at fiscal stimulation to increase employment beyond that rate were invariably inflationary.

Monetarists taught that the supply of money was the product of the stock of money—just the sum of spendable coin, bills, checking accounts, etc.—times its turnover rate, or its *velocity*. Friedman's historical research showed that velocity was highly stable, so government policy need concern itself only with the money stock. If the Federal Reserve expanded the money stock at approximately the rate of economic growth, prices would also stay roughly constant. Most important of all, given Friedman's antipathy to activist government, a rigid rule for monetary management conceivably might replace the Federal Reserve with a computer. (Friedman opposed almost all forms of government regulation, including safety regulations for pharmaceuticals.)

Both the Keynesian and monetarist constructs immediately flunk the Popper/Soros test of falsifiability. The practical differences between them are highly nuanced, and the data of economics, after all, has nothing like the precision of the data of real sciences. If one tries to tease out the actual effect of specific policies, the trail almost always trickles away into a cloud of statistical white noise.* One lesson of the monetarist experiment, moreover, is a

---

* For example, the Kennedy recovery came at a time when international trade was booming, and all industrial economies were growing rapidly, most faster than America, and his signature intervention, the 1964 tax cut, was passed only after the economy had already resumed growth. Chicago School acolytes make

kind of Heisenberg principle of economic intervention. Once
policy makers focus their regulatory attention on a specific variable,
like the stock of money, its actual relation to all other variables will
be changed beyond recognition. That was a lesson that Paul
Volcker learned to his pain when he attempted to apply monetarist
principles in the early 1980s.

REAL-LIFE EXPERIMENTS

Soros's practical experience as a broker and research analyst convinced him that the normal market state was, in fact, disequilibrium.
His own assumption of disequilibrium, Soros acknowledges, is as
unfalsifiable as any other economic theory. As an investor, however,
he finds it more useful than an assumption of market rationality,
because it is a better pointer to profit opportunities. Two of his
early investment successes were crucial to the evolution of his
thinking.

The first was related to the conglomerate movement in the second half of the 1960s. The flurry of company takeovers, Soros
saw, merely exploited investors' tendency to rate companies by
trends in earnings per share (EPS). Start with modestly sized Company A, and engineer a debt-financed acquisition of B, a much

---

similar claims for targeted tax cuts for owners of capital, which similarly dissolve
upon close analysis. While government economic policies can be important, they
are frequently overwhelmed by larger trends. For example, Robert Rubin, Treasury
secretary through most of the Clinton administration, attributes the high growth
of the late 1990s to a 1993 tax increase; but other forces, like boomers reaching
their high-output, high-saving forties and fifties, the microprocessor and Internet
revolution, and huge social security surpluses, dwarfed any traceable impact from
the tax change.

larger, stodgy company with stagnant revenues, a modest EPS, and a low market price. Merge B into A, and retire B's stock, and the resulting combined A/B will have a much higher debt load, but a much smaller stock base. So long as B's earnings more than cover the new debt service, the combined A/B will show a huge jump in per-share revenues and earnings. Uncritical investors then push up A/B's stock price, which helps finance new acquisitions. Jim Ling was one of the early exploiters of the strategy, parlaying a modest Dallas electronics company into a sprawling giant with dozens of companies, spanning everything from steel to avionics, meatpacking, and golf balls.

Business schools justified the scam by theorizing that conglomerates deserved higher share prices because their diversified business mix would deliver smoother and steadier earnings. It was the kind of dumb idea that underscores the disconnect between business schools and real business. If shareholders want earnings diversification, of course, they can quickly and easily diversify stock portfolios in the market. Big conglomerates, in fact, probably warrant *lower* stock prices. They're hard to manage, are often run by financial operators, and usually carry outsized debt loads.

Soros understood that the conglomerate game made no sense, but he also recognized its strong following among market professionals. "I respect the herd," he told me, not because it's right, but because "it's like the ocean."[5] Even the stupidest idea may warrant investment, in other words, if it has a grip on the market's imagination. So Soros invested heavily in conglomerates, riding up the stock curve until he sensed it was nearing a top. Then he took his winnings and switched to the short side, enjoying a second huge payday on the way down.

As the conglomerate boom was collapsing, he saw a second boom shaping up in real estate investment trusts, or REITs. A REIT is a limited partnership that invests in real estate. The rapid growth of REITs, like most bubbles, had a basis in reality—among other things, the demographic shift from the old manufacturing centers of the Northeast and Middle West to the Sun Belt states necessarily presaged a construction and development boom.

But Soros also calculated that the REIT financial structure would feed a propensity for overvaluation. He outlined the arithmetic in a widely distributed 1970 research memo. Assume a REIT with a book value of $10 a share, earning a 12 percent return. As the product gains popularity, it raises another $10 million at $20 a share. Assuming it still earns 12 percent on its investments, its total book value is now $20 million, the value per share jumps from $10 to $13.33, and earnings per share from $1.20 to $1.60,* even though the return on capital is unchanged. Much as in the conglomerate bubble, Soros forecast that so long as real estate markets stayed frothy, REITs would outperform, until either a glut of REIT investment or some other reversal popped the bubble.

For an agile investor like Soros, REITs were nearly ideal—a bubble in a relatively "static disequilibrium," one that could persist

---

* The arithmetic: Assume the original REIT has 1 million shares at $10 per share, or $10 million book value, with 12 percent annual income = $1.2 million, or $1.20 share. It then raises an additional $10 million at $20 a share, issuing 500,000 new shares and investing at the same 12 percent rate of return. The book value of the shares is now $20 million/1.5 million shares = $13.33 per share. (Note that the second round of shareholders paid a premium over book.) Its earnings are 12 percent on $20 million, or $2.4 million. Dividing by 1.5 million shares = $1.60 per share. The calculations are from the example in Soros's REIT memo.

for a long period of time. So he could enjoy a long ride up the curve, with plenty of time to see the crash coming, and then enjoy a long ride down. As he did during the conglomerate boom, he invested heavily in the early stages of the REIT wave, took his profits near the market high, then exited for a few years until the industry started to struggle. He started selling short "more or less indiscriminately,"[6] riding the collapse all the way down, making at least as much as he had on the way up.

"Bubbles are like trees," he told me. "It takes time for them to take their full, beautiful shapes. But bubbles are just one element in markets. In forests, a tree almost never takes its natural shape, because it's hemmed in by so many other trees."[7] He put REITs in the rare but highly desirable class of bubbles that evolve their true "beautiful" shape.

MAKING SENSE OF BUBBLES

Soros was intuitively convinced that the notion of markets as a hyperrational optimization machine was wrong, but he struggled to understand *why*, to make philosophic sense of the intuition. The key, he finally decided, was the concept of *reflexivity*, which has played a key role in his thinking every since. There can never be a hard science about human behavior, he reasoned, because we interact unpredictably with other humans—our behavior is *reflexive*, the product of multiple unpredictable mutual interactions, with none of the law-governed regularities of physics.

Financial markets, however, occupy an ambiguous position between the world of hard science and the reflexive world of humans. In settled times, markets frequently do appear to be governed by law-like statistical rules, which enamor economic modelers. But those regularities break down dramatically in times of stress because of the reflexive, or mutual, interaction between human expectations and actual market behavior. It was the herd's bullishness on REITs that drove REIT prices into bubbledom, or "boom-and-bust" in Soros's terminology, with each round of share price increases fueling expectations for more in a self-amplifying spiral until the bubble finally popped. Then a reverse phenomenon took over on the way down, assuring an overshoot on that side as well.

When reflexivity tends to dominate, Soros reasoned, unsettled markets are ripe for bubble formation. But while reflexivity might be a necessary condition for bubbles, it wasn't sufficient. Boom-and-bust cycles almost always involve credit, and normally don't get underway in the absence of fundamental misperceptions about credit. Lenders misperceive the creditworthiness of borrowers, or the future values of assets like houses. As they increase their lending, asset prices indeed rise, confirming their original conviction, so they increase their lending even further, even as their success draws in even more lenders, until a full boom-and-bust cycle ensues.

Bubbles are being created all the time, he says, but most are choked off before they build up much momentum. During his investing career, he guesses there were only "six to ten" long-run bubbles, plus an overall "superbubble" in credit and debt that he estimates has been inflating since the end of the last world war.

Reflexivity and the frequency of bubbles, plus the fact that they can grow to explosive scale, exposes the fatuity of Chicago School dogma about "efficient" self-regulating markets. "After all," Soros said, "if markets are so efficient, why are they always breaking down?"[8] He might have added, "And how could it be possible for me to make so much money betting that they will?"

SOROS THE INVESTOR

Reflexivity for Soros is less a guide to strategies than a useful divining rod for turning up opportunities. There is a rich gold seam of reflexivity in the zone where market players interact with government regulators. As Soros put it, "The relationship between financial authorities and financial markets is an ongoing reflexive process. Both act with imperfect knowledge, and both are subject to the disparity between reality and perceptions of reality. That's endemic. So this interplay between markets and the authorities is one that I really used to focus on."[9]

The vast economic disruptions of the 1970s offered splendid opportunities to an investor like Soros, and his Quantum Fund's* returns soared. One of the key developments was a credit bubble, which he had anticipated in a shrewd 1972 memo, "The Case for Growth Banking." Led by Citibank (then First National City Bank), banks were for the first time trying to drive up their stock price to finance expansion into new products and markets, and to support steady increases in leverage. It eventuated, in Soros's

---

* Soros's investment company is Soros Funds Management. The Quantum Fund has been its primary investment vehicle for the past forty years. The fund contracts with the management company for investment services in return for a fee of 1 percent of assets plus 20 percent of profits. Most of the fees accrued to Soros personally, since he was the dominant owner of the management company. Since he always left his profits in the fund, his personal share of the fund grew steadily.

paradigm, in a classic boom-and-bust cycle that terminated with the Mexican debt crisis of 1982. In a broader view, Soros sees the period as just an episode in a sixty-year credit superbubble that the violent credit unwinding of 2008 and 2009 may finally be bringing to a close.

To convey a flavor of the mechanics of Soros's investing, however, I will summarize two well-documented episodes that capture the extraordinary breadth and depth of his approach to markets. The first is drawn from a fifteen-month investment diary he maintained in the mid-1980s while working on his magnum opus, *The Alchemy of Finance* (1987); the second is the famous 1992 episode when he earned a ten-figure profit from almost single-handedly forcing the devaluation of the British pound.

THE IMPERIAL CIRCLE

The investment diary covers August 1985 through October 1986, during a time that Soros calls Ronald Reagan's "Imperial Circle." After runaway inflation was crushed in 1982, the economy veered into a peculiar growth stage that most economists regarded as highly unstable. Soros had much the same view at the diary's start, but he modified it considerably in the ensuing months. He considered the growth economy of the mid-1980s to be in a highly reflexive state because its success was tightly intertwined with the positive international impression of Ronald Reagan's presidential leadership and the dramatic recovery of American political and economic power.[10]

The post-inflation economy of the 1980s was an unusual blend of strong growth and a strong dollar, but with big trade and budget deficits. According to conventional wisdom, it was unsustainable—strong currencies don't coexist with big deficits. But the circle was squared by high American interest rates. High rates sucked in capital from abroad, so foreigners financed the U.S. trade deficits. At the same time, the depressive effect of high interest rates at home was offset by the big budget deficits. So, while high dollar interest rates imposed crushing burdens on developing countries like Brazil and Mexico, they helped America live comfortably beyond its means. That was the Imperial Circle.

But there were worrying underlying trends. The concurrent boom in American financial markets was mostly related to company takeovers—Soros called it "Mergermania." In effect, investment capital was being channeled away from plant and productive equipment toward financial instruments. That was pleasant in the near term, for the increased financial liquidity offset high interest rates and supported consumption growth. But it also presaged a dangerous shift away from producing tradable goods toward a purely finance-driven economy.*

---

* The key elements of the Imperial Circle stayed in place for twenty-plus years. The extended duration of the 1985–2005 credit bubble is the major reason why its current unwinding is so devastating. There was one important change from the 1980s dispensation to the more recent one. Interest rates fell sharply in the United States starting in the mid-1990s, which should have choked off the inflow of foreign capital. But it was replaced by interest-insensitive capital from export-driven nations like China that bought American bonds to supply liquidity to American consumers. Starting in the mid-1990s, academics began to acknowledge the possibility of a new quasi-equilibrium under the general rubric of a "Bretton Woods II" regime. At least a decade earlier, Soros had perceived the system's ramifications and was among the first to worry about the concentration on finance.

The Soros investing style that emerges from the diary is striking, the more so since it is from the era when he is still running money more or less by himself. He moves very quickly and in very large amounts, investing, he later wrote, as if the Quantum Fund were his own money, adding, "which it is to a large extent." Since he was the sole investment manager, he thought of it as a unified platform instead of separate equity, fixed-income, and currency businesses. Major decisions usually involved adjusting the whole fund. Soros uses leverage (borrowed money) freely, but within rules of thumb that are adjusted flexibly to adapt to his current world view. He usually executes large movements in stocks with indexes, but may later reallocate among particular sectors.

His investing is always emphatically global; in the 1980s he could generally use the United States, Germany, and Japan as a reasonable proxy for the industrial countries. The point of view is always holistic, so a decision on German securities typically had implications for his American and Japanese holdings. The instruments of choice are opportunistic—whatever is the most efficient way to achieve a position. So in this period, he invested in stocks, bonds, currencies, and commodities from all three main countries and often others, taking both long and short positions. His hedges often involved very distant instruments, so he might offset a long position in U.S. bonds with short positions in Japan—in other words, he looks for rough, directional hedges rather than precisely calculated offsets.

His investments always have an underlying theory—which he recognizes might often be wrong. If he can't plausibly describe the underlying market dynamics, however, he stays out. While his investing paradigm—the concepts of reflexivity, bubbles, and

the like—stays constant, his investing hypotheses can change almost as often as his positions. He stays acutely aware of developments on the political side—in the 1980s, trying to divine the
chances of an international dollar-stabilization accord, any movement toward American-Soviet détente, or whether Congress might
rein in the budget deficit.

Finally, the tone of the diary is dyspeptic to an extreme—constantly railing at himself, reciting litanies of mistakes and wrong
turns, lists of obvious missed inflection points, one stupid loss
after another. But when the diary breaks the narrative to add things
up, you discover that he's been racking up huge profits.

Soros opens the diary with a brief assessment of the investing
climate. He is happy with James Baker as the new Treasury secretary, since he appears to understand the dangers of the Imperial
Circle. The indications are that he is trying to chart a "soft landing"
scenario that might involve an orderly decline in the dollar, a re-
bound in American exports, and more balanced economic growth.
The alternative is a "disaster scenario" whereby the dollar stays
strong for an extended period and then plunges precipitately. Soros
worries that a harsh recession could cause the Fed to inject liquidity
and lose control of inflation.

Without great conviction, he expects credit contraction. The
stock market and housing markets are both weakening, banks are
in serious trouble, and currencies are pushing against their upper
bounds. On the positive side, the budget deficit is falling along
with interest rates, and banks are slowly improving their balance
sheets. What to do?

He decides to bet on recession. He takes a "maximum position"
in currencies, shorting dollars and buying marks, and he goes

short U.S. bonds, since he expects that a falling dollar will force an increase in long-term American interest rates. (Bond prices fall when rates rise.) He is long on the yen but isn't concerned about it, since Japan is clearly managing its currency to maintain its American trade surplus. He increases his already large short positions in oil, since the oil cartel is disintegrating, and he expects the Saudis to reassert control by launching a price war. Recession will add to those pressures.

After about three weeks, he concludes that he's gotten almost all of it wrong, except his oil bet. The dollar jumps on surprisingly good economic reports—Soros doesn't trust them but isn't prepared to fight them. Bonds rise at the same time but quickly drop back. Then he compounds his mistakes by making the exactly wrong trade. He closes out the bond shorts just before bonds drop, but holds on to his long positions in currencies as they also drop. He decides not to fight the market until he gets a clearer view. Nervously, he maintains his long position in marks although he expects a saw-toothed trading pattern that will test his resolve.

Nearly three weeks later, he is spectacularly bailed out by the "Group of Five"—the finance ministers and central bankers of the United States, Germany, France, Great Britain, and Japan. At an emergency meeting at New York's Plaza Hotel, they agree to shift from freely floating exchange rates to a system of "managed" floating within preset bands. The objective is to push down the dollar, thereby vindicating all of Soros's currency bets, which he still had in place "by the skin of his teeth." He makes a killing on his mark holdings, and because he instantly grasps that the yen will also rise, he scoops up big yen positions and makes a killing there too. But the fretting kicks back in almost immediately—

more worries about American banks,* losses on his oil shorts (there was unrest in the Gulf), and losses on a brief long position in American stocks.

Soros closes out his oil shorts, but otherwise sits still for a couple of weeks. Then in late October, he starts reducing his dollar shorts and buying dollars. Soros is an extremely active trader. He hasn't changed his negative view of the dollar, but he expects a brief technical market reversal, and wants to take advantage. He's wrong—Japan announces a surprise rate increase, which triggers dollar selling in favor of yen. But his short positions in Texas and California banks look like winning offsets. Overall, however, he's done very well. Since mid-August, the fund is up more than $100 million, a 17 percent gain in ten weeks.

November is relatively quiet. Soros reestablishes his currency positions and goes long in stocks and bonds, griping that he misses the turn in each market. But when he lays out the numbers, you discover he's been doing fine. It dawns that when Soros complains about missing a market, he usually means that he failed to move before the markets turned. But even when he doesn't anticipate

---

* With reason: The biggest American banks were actually insolvent through most of the 1980s due to losses on their "petrodollar" loans. OPEC nations had deposited most of their massive oil earnings in American banks' overseas branches. Brimming with interest-bearing deposits, the banks chose the fastest way to convert them to earning assets—by making huge loans to developing countries, primarily in Latin America, nominally "guaranteed" by the borrowing country governments. When the loans defaulted en masse, the U.S. financial authorities expressly decided to fake the books—treating all the petrodollar loans as "performing" when they were virtually all in default. The charade continued until the end of the decade, when the expedient of the "Brady Bonds" allowed the loans to be written off and countries like Mexico and Brazil to reenter the capital markets.

turning points, his reactions are so fast and he moves in such volume that he captures premium returns anyway—all the teeth-
grinding is just that they might have been even higher.

In December 1985, Soros takes a pause from his investing
chronicle and updates his market view, which is characteristically
acute. He now sees a greater possibility of a graceful transition
away from the Imperial Circle, largely because of sensible policy
moves—the Plaza agreement to lower the dollar, the possibility of
tough congressional "Gramm-Rudman" deficit restrictions, and
the move toward international détente. He also, correctly, expects
the government to shift from fiscal (spending) stimulus to monetary
stimulus—which, in fact, became standard policy throughout the
twelve-year reign of the Fed's new chairman, Alan Greenspan.

Despite the surge in lending for takeover deals, Soros believes
that credit is actually contracting. Leveraged buyouts, he argues,
depress the economy. Junk-bond yields tend to pull up interest
rates, while corporate cash flows are siphoned into debt service
rather than physical investment, pulling down productivity.

His ideal case is that rising stock prices will choke off the
takeover boom, investment will shift back to physical assets, consumers will start shoring up their savings, and American international imbalances will be worked down. But he sees lots of obsta-
cles—housing and consumer credit are getting very loose, the
banks are still awash in bad international debt, the coming collapse
in oil prices could be disruptive.

With intended irony, he dubs one of the likely bad outcomes
as a return to the "golden age of capitalism," meaning the tooth-
and-claw capitalism of the nineteenth century. That could happen,
he fears, if the government withdraws from its efforts to manage

the dollar down and constrain financial excesses. It would increase the staying power of the Imperial Circle, and allow the imbalances to continue to build. "[U]ntrammeled free enterprise has produced horrendous results in the past," he writes. "Are we to repeat the same experience again? Hopefully not. . . . The fatal flaw of a free market system is its inherent instability."

If the Imperial Circle does stay in place, however, he expects that in the short term there could be "the bull market of a lifetime." Although he regards the long-term consequences of prolonging the status quo to be quite dire, he will position himself to draw maximum profits from it. In mid-December, the fund is up to $890 million, a 37 percent gain since the diary's August starting point and 80 percent for all of 1985.

The diary continues through October 1986. His trading pattern remains much the same—he maintains an overarching investing thesis, but still makes very rapid moves into and out of markets in pursuit of slight market realignments. The short-term moves often don't work out, but since his macro take on the market is roughly correct, his overall outcomes continue to be strong.

He opens January, for instance, long in most instruments, operating on his "bull market of a lifetime" hypothesis, then decides he's overleveraged and pulls back sharply—just in time to miss a major market surge, to much self-flagellation. Of course, he doesn't really miss the turn; it's just that he would have made even more with the riskier positioning.

And here is a priceless entry from April:

> The market flip-flopped in the last two days and so did I. On
> Monday, oil rallied sharply, and bonds, stocks, and currencies

sold off; on Tuesday, all these markets reversed themselves. The move on Monday hurt me on all fronts. I discovered how sensitive my portfolio was to oil prices; I also discovered that there was more leverage in it than I thought. I had neglected my [mark/pound] cross position, which turned against me with a vengeance. To quantify it, I dropped a cool $100 million from the onset of the correction.

That sounds disastrous. When he sums up his accounts the next month, however, the fund is approaching $1.4 billion, the per share gain is more than 110 percent since the diary's start, and 45 percent since the beginning of the year. The secret, he later explains, is very large gains in equity positions, which are "too far afield" to discuss in detail, involving Finnish shares, Japanese railroads and real estate, and Hong Kong real estate.

July and August of 1986 are very stressful. His portfolio is still positioned according to the "bull market of a lifetime" scenario, but he's worried by a potential deflationary spiral triggered by a total collapse in oil prices. He explains, "As a general principle, I do not dismantle positions that are built on a thesis that remains valid; rather, I take additional positions in the opposite direction on the basis of the new thesis. The result is a delicate balance that needs to be adjusted from moment to moment."

Within a few days he builds a complicated edifice of Japanese and American stocks and bonds that should give him maximum flexibility. But he still complains that he is late to reposition, and "my posture is liable to change from minute to minute. I shall have to be much more active and nimble."

By the end of August, he is beginning to relax. His rebalancing strategy has worked out very well, and he is now reducing his leverage for safety, intentionally taking some losses in doing so. Overall, his performance has been spectacular. The fund is up to $1.6 billion; the August to August per share gain is 142 percent.

But markets are humbling, even for Soros. August is the high point of the diary period. In September, he is caught in a nasty market break, and reports ruefully, "[It was a] sharp contrast with the July/August break, which I managed to dodge successfully. In a sense, I was faked out by that break. Hedging against it left me emotionally exhausted, and when the more severe break came I was asleep at the switch."

Those losses were real, costing more than $100 million in just a couple of days. For the remainder of the diary through October 1986, he is intentionally less active. He loses on a bet that a German-American financial accord will be reached but decides to increase his position because he expects a deal will be struck quietly anyway. He takes an extended trip to China, but cuts it short when his Japanese equity and real estate positions deteriorate sharply. He senses correctly that Japan may be on the brink of a long decline, and laments that he didn't spot it earlier.

There is also a prescient entry in October, in which he worries about the rise of program trading and portfolio insurance, which was a major factor in the "Black Monday" stock market a year later. In the final diary tally, his fund is just under $1.5 billion, up 112 percent per share since the August start date, fifteen months before.

The 1992 episode involving the British pound is much more straightforward but is a splendid example of Soros's consummate boldness.

"THE MAN WHO BROKE THE BANK OF ENGLAND"

Currency regimes, in Soros's perspective, are rich mines of reflexivity, since they frequently evolve as contests of perception between traders and governments. In today's highly integrated markets, most governments try to manage their exchange rate to prevent disruptive fluctuations in the price of traded goods.* But once an exchange rate is fixed, it is a natural target for speculators, who constantly probe a government's resolve.

At bottom, a proper exchange rate is determined by the home country economy. So long as it has a record of solid growth and modest inflation, and maintains adequate reserves, foreigners will be inclined to hold its currency, but if economic policies veer off track, they will demand to be paid in reserve currencies, usually the dollar, the euro, or the yen. At some point, traders will start selling currency futures in anticipation of a devaluation. If traders take dollars for the promise to deliver a fixed amount of rubles a month from now, they will make large profits if the dollar value of rubles falls in the meantime.

---

* According to Chicago School free-market theorists, efficient markets should ensure that exchange rates adjust smoothly in small increments. As the doctrine gained influence in the 1980s, most larger countries shifted to free-floating regimes. The theory was wrong. Instead of stabilizing adjustments, violent seesawing was much more common.

Great Britain chose to join the European Rate Mechanism (ERM) in 1990. The ERM had been adopted in 1979 to reduce exchange rate disparities as part of the agenda to move toward a currency union among the Common Market countries. Members agreed to maintain their currencies within a mutual reference band of +/-2.25 percent of the initial rates. As a practical matter, since Germany had the lowest inflation and the strongest reserve position, participating countries were fixing their currency against the mark. Member countries were implicitly also committing to raise interest rates or dampen inflation if their currencies approached the lower end of the band.[11]

The strains on the ERM in the early 1990s can be traced to the reunification of Germany after the fall of the Berlin Wall. To ease reunification trauma for East Germans, West Germany chose to peg the East's nominal wages and incomes to western marks, despite very low East German productivity. The consequence was a huge, and badly underforecast, income transfer from west to east, estimated at 4 to 5 percent of western GDP, and more than a third of eastern GDP. Since German politicians did not dare raise taxes by that amount, they financed the subsidies by borrowing. To offset the inflationary impact of such a massive stimulus, the head of the German Bundesbank, Helmut Schlesinger, engineered a sharp rise in interest rates. The rest of the ERM countries had no choice but to follow suit, although most of them were already sliding into recession.* A British backbencher said that ERM stood for "Eternal Recession Machine."

---

* The United States has a well-deserved reputation for making its currency policy hostage to domestic political considerations, thus defaulting on its crucial responsibility as manager of the world's primary reserve currency. Germany is typically just as irresponsible but is less criticized because its anti-inflationary

By the summer of 1992, with the rate crunch biting ever deeper, speculating against ERM currencies was essentially a bet on the willingness of governments to endure unemployment for the sake of a currency agreement. Traders concentrated on Italy first, scoring a big win when Italy devalued by 7 percent on September 13.

Attention shifted to Great Britain. The pound had been under pressure all summer, falling more than 4 percent against the dollar. But the Tory prime minister, John Major, was determined to hold the line. The Treasury borrowed $14.3 billion in marks in early September and bought pounds aggressively in foreign exchange markets. In a weak gesture of solidarity, the German government lowered its bank rate by a risible quarter point, to 9.5 percent, on September 15. Such a pallid action, along with an accompanying statement from Schlesinger emphasizing the dangers of inflation, only encouraged speculators.

On September 16, known in Britain as "Black Wednesday," the Bank of England pushed up its own discount rate from 10 percent to 12 percent, and promised to go to 15 percent if necessary. With a public already outraged by a harsh British recession, it wasn't credible. A global wave of pound sales overwhelmed the British defenses. It "suspended" its membership in the ERM, and the pound quickly dropped about 10 percent. From that point, the ERM was effectively a dead letter.

Soros's central role in the attack on the pound wasn't revealed until late October. The original idea for attacking the pound came

---

bias is cast as the path of virtue. Its 1990s policies, however, condemned much of Europe to prolonged quasi-recession, and it may be repeating that behavior in 2009.

from Stanley Druckenmiller, whom Soros recruited from Dreyfus, and in 1989 put in charge of the day-to-day management of the Quantum Fund. Soros stayed closely in touch but, as he later put it, was more of a "coach" than the manager on the spot. Druckenmiller naturally reviewed big positions with him, however. When he presented his idea, Soros agreed immediately, but insisted that any move had to be on a very large scale.

Soros generally does not trade in currency future markets, in part because it's almost impossible to conceal large positions. For the pound gambit, he and Druckenmiller quietly lined up pound credit lines at banks around the world. Since he was the ultimate counterparty, banks were happy to create the lines. In all, he lined up $10 billion in credit, at perhaps one hundred different bank branches, under many different local account names.

Soros had attended an investment conference a few weeks earlier, where Schlesinger, both in his prepared remarks and in a brief conversation afterward, gave Soros a strong impression that Germany would not intervene in currency markets to support the pound.* Nothing Schlesinger said on the fifteenth contradicted that. So when the British made their desperate 2 percent rate hike the next day, which Soros viewed as an "admission of defeat,"[12] he pulled the trigger—simultaneously drawing all the pound lines

---

* I once asked Soros if any of his success was based on information that wouldn't be available to other investors. He said no, which was my impression, but he came back to the question later. He had become an "insider" in the 1970s in the sense that he could speak to central bankers; at one point, Soros was taking as much as 7 percent of British bond issues. "If you can ask a central banker a question and see his color change, then you do have a kind of inside information," he said.

and selling them in exchange for marks. Faced with a sudden tsunami of pound sales from around the world, virtually all of the world's traders started dumping their positions. By itself, the Soros onslaught might have exhausted the remainder of the British mark reserves, but as the whole trading community grabbed the wave, the British had no choice but to cave, which happened within hours. Norman Lamont, Chancellor of the Exchequer, later said that he would have been willing to buy as much as $15 billion worth of pounds in the market. Soros said, "And I would have been willing to buy it all."[13]

The immediate fall in the pound was about 10 percent. That night, as Soros slept soundly in New York, the Quantum traders simply reexchanged their marks for the now-cheaper pounds they had sold the previous day, and paid off the bank lines. Soros conceded that his sterling profits were approximately $1 billion, and says that his total winnings, including related bets like his long position in British bonds, roughly doubled that total.

In truth, it wasn't much of a gamble—"It was an asymmetric position," he told me.[14] The British were clearly at the end of their tether on the ERM. The electorate was Europhobic in the best of times, and in a state of outrage by rate hikes in the teeth of a recession. Defending the currency with more rate hikes would have likely brought down the government. And Soros's actual financial risks were fairly modest. If the British had somehow held the line on pound/mark rates, Soros would have repurchased his pounds for approximately what he had paid for them, perhaps a tad more, and paid back his lines. The maximum loss might have been $100 million, which, while not trivial, is hardly catastrophic for a $3 billion fund. Stacked up against an excellent chance to bank a billion overnight, it was an easy bet.

In retrospect, Soros tends to minimize Quantum's role. He is pretty sure that the government and the trading community knew that Quantum had triggered the move, which would have mitigated its impact. He also points out that he was far from the only factor in the market when the British finally folded.

Perhaps. But the fact remains that Soros's role in the crisis was unknown until the *London Daily Mail* picked up a report, apparently from a New York hedge fund tracking service based on a quarterly position report that Quantum had filed in the Netherlands Antilles. The *Mail* report unleashed a brief frenzy in the British press, prompting Soros to give a full account of the episode to a friendly London *Times* reporter.[15]

In truth, if officials and traders had thought Soros was behind the coup against the pound, the insider buzz could not have been hushed up. The financial press is quick to pick up trader gossip, especially in so prominent an episode, and angry government officials are avid leakers.

Even if the government did know that the initial surge was just Soros, it wouldn't have made a difference. The whole strategy was calculated for maximum shock, precisely to ensure massive me-too selling and official panic. (Given the market chaos, it's hard to imagine Treasury officials coolly recommending, "This looks like mostly Soros; let's see if we can wait him out.")

Was it an antisocial act? It's hard to see why. German domestic priorities had long since put the ERM under unbearable strain. Only the stubbornness of politicians had kept it in place for so long. And as soon as the pound stabilized at a defensible level, British bank rates were reduced, and exports picked up smartly. From 1990 through 1992, real British GDP had dropped by 1.2 percent. But over the three years following the devaluation, real growth averaged a sparkling 3.2 percent. Half of Soros's total profits from the pound devaluation, after all, came from his bets on precisely such a recovery.

In short, by accelerating the inevitable, Soros did the British a favor. The man in the street, indeed, may have thought as much. By most accounts, once the initial shock of the revelation had worn off, British public attitudes toward Soros were quite admiring.

SUMMING UP THE RECORD

Soros's stunning investment results speak for themselves. What is most impressive, however, is how he got them: the vast range of his positions, the seemingly frenetic moves into and out of very complex investment constructs, and the seamless way Quantum's investment profile morphs to track subtle shifts in his world view. When Michael Kaufman, author of the most detailed Soros biography, asked Soros's colleagues and peers about his secret, they spoke of an "almost mystical . . . ability to visualize the entire world's money and credit flows." Gary Gladstein, his longtime administrative and financial chief, said, "He consumes all this information, digests it all, and from there he can come out with his opinion as to how this is all going to be sorted out. What the impact will be on the dollar or other currencies, the interest rate markets. He'll look at charts, but most of the information he's processing is verbal, not statistical." Soros said something similar to me—that in the years when he was most intensely involved with the fund, "the fund and my brain were interchangeable."[16]

The strategies were rarely articulated—they changed too often—and were largely intuitive. At one point in *Alchemy*, he muses about whether spelling out his strategies for the diary is hurting his performance because it makes him more committed to sticking with them. In published conversations with Byron Wien, the former chief investment strategist for Morgan Stanley, and the European journalist Krisztina Koenen, Soros stressed that he had no interest in modern portfolio theory. "We live in the Stone Age," he said, "deliberately so"—and went on to explain that all modern portfolio math assumed benign equilibria, while he was more interested in market "discontinuities," the points where so-called efficient markets broke down.[17]

Soros's son Robert made a famous comment on the role of theory and intuition in Soros's investing—and Soros repeated it to me:

> My father will sit down and give you theories to explain why he does this or that. But I remember seeing it as a kid and thinking, Jesus Christ, at least half of this is bullshit. I mean, you know the reason he changes his position on the market or whatever is because his back starts killing him. It has nothing to do with reason. He literally goes into a spasm and it's this early warning sign.[18]

Soros is acutely aware of the limitations of the most useful theories as a practical investing guide. At one point in his *Alchemy* diary, he notes that his travel schedule may be the most important factor in his performance, and lists all the economic forecasts that he got wrong. A great deal of his 1985 success hinged on the timing of the Plaza agreement, which saved his long currency positions. But by the time he published the diary, he had learned how close that agreement had come to breaking down. Fifteen years later, reviewing his performance after the Asian currency crisis of the late 1990s, he decided that he was betrayed by a too-rigid adherence to his own theories. In particular, he was much too bearish on the prospects of Asian recoveries, because he had fallen in love with his boom-and-bust model: "I rode what had been a fertile fallacy into exhaustion."[19]

Druckenmiller, who was chief trader and strategist at Quantum for twelve years and had as close a working relationship with Soros as anyone, listed the intangibles that make Soros such a great investor. For one thing, he is a "magnificent loss taker. He just gets rid of it and doesn't worry about his ego or what the world is going to say." Soros was on the wrong side of the stock market during the 1987 October Black Monday crash—he was expecting it to hit Japan first—and took huge losses. His response was to sell everything he had, to hootings from the financial press that he was just locking in his losses. Within a week or so, however, he had shifted to a huge leveraged dollar short, and finished the year with a 15 percent gain.

There are a lot of analysts who can divine markets, Druckenmiller says, but Soros is unmatched at "going for the jugular," for "pulling the trigger." "Pulling the trigger," Druckenmiller said, "is not about analysis; it's not about predicting trends. . . . [It means] to be willing at the right moment in time to put it all on the line. That is not something, in my opinion, that can be learned. It is totally intuitive, and it is an art, not in any way a science." Druckenmiller cites the 1992 pound sterling episode. After he described the strategy to Soros, he said he got "something close to a scolding, which was, well, if you believe all that, why are you betting only two or three billion." Similarly, after Soros made his huge currency gains in the wake of the Plaza Agreement, he was upset to find his traders locking in the profits. The big hit was still to come. Instead of taking profits, he piled in even bigger. The fund was up 122 percent that year.

Druckenmiller sums up: Soros "developed the hedge fund model and he managed a fund longer and more successfully than anyone so far. It's one thing to do this for five or ten years. But to have the stamina to do it really well [for such a long time] is incredible. . . . He is the standard."[20]

Soros and his funds navigated the late 1990s Asian currency crises in good shape, although because of the 1992 experience, he was regularly accused of provoking it, especially by the Malaysian prime minister, Mahathir Mohamad. In fact, Soros was buying ringgits when the crisis broke. He had sold long-dated ringgit futures prior to the devaluation, and was buying on the slide—prematurely he conceded—to lock in his profits. (That earlier selling, of course, would have contributed to the slide, but the movement was general, and Soros wasn't a prime mover as in the pound episode.) For Soros, however, the Asian crises confirmed his view of the inherent instability of financial markets. In theory, rational markets should have smoothed the course of a transition in currency regimes. Instead markets turned into a "wrecking ball" that swung from economy to economy, some of which, like Hong Kong's, were quite sound but were almost destroyed in the backdrafts.[21]

Finally, although Soros had stayed clear of the Western plunge into the late-1990s Russian financial boom, he allowed certain of the Soros funds to participate. (With $6 billion under management, Soros Funds was no longer the tightly controlled entity it had been a decade before.) He himself was extremely hopeful for Russia's future, but his growing foundation-based activities in Russia made him wary of appearances of conflicts. With some trepidation, he finally made a major investment in a newly privatized Russian telephone company—after all, he had long preached the importance of private capital to the reconstruction of Russia. Sadly, what could have been a successful venture precipitated a vicious battle for control among rival gangs of oligarchs. "I was naïve," he summed up.[22] The gang war continues still, in his view, although now it is between the oligarchs and the *siloviki*, the "hard men" from the KGB who have taken over the government with Vladimir Putin.

Druckenmiller was exhausted by the currency crises and retired from Soros Funds in 2000. Soros was seventy by then, with no appetite for plunging back into funds management full time. Instead, he reconfigured his funds into a variety of conservatively managed investment vehicles that would require little of his personal oversight. As the recent credit crunch loomed, however, he returned to primary management of Soros Funds in 2007. He clearly still had the touch. He was one of the top performers and earners in 2007, with personal earnings of $2.9 billion, and again, in the very difficult year of 2008, racking up a cool $1.1 billion.[23]

Now well into his eighth decade, Soros has become a true world figure. As a young man in London, working odd jobs and trying to get into university, he still regarded himself as something of a "messianic" and "godlike" figure—his words—almost relishing that he was at the very bottom of the British pecking order, because of his conviction that he would somehow get to the very top.

His advice is now eagerly sought on public issues, most particularly, of course, on the current financial crisis. His books—he has written nine in all—are frequently best sellers, and his commentary regularly appears in the leading financial press. His stature is enhanced by the major philanthropic role he has played over the past thirty years. Unlike many financiers, he can also speak from a deep understanding of poverty, inequality, and injustice. Therefore, before we turn to his recommendations for dealing with the current financial crisis, herewith a brief sketch of his philanthropies.

THE PHILANTHROPIST

Soros was in mid-career, just on the verge of his greatest earnings years when he first dipped his toe into philanthropy, but within twenty years he was overseeing one of the most prominent, and arguably one of the most successful, foundations in the world. His very prominent role in accelerating the process of de-Sovietization of central Europe made him a major player on the world stage. Morton Abramowitz, director of the Carnegie Endowment for International Peace, called him "the only man in the United States who has his own foreign policy and can implement it."[24]

His initial forays were those of the typical wealthy New Yorker—grants to modern dance companies, refurbishing Central Park. By the end of the 1970s, however, nearing fifty, completing a divorce, making a great deal of money, and for the first time thinking through what he wanted to do for the rest of his life, he began to think about philanthropy in a more systematic way, and decided to commit $3 million a year to philanthropic causes.

Just as in investing, however, Soros didn't like to make a major move without a hypothesis—what was the purpose of his philanthropy? He came up with the answer by using the same Popperist lens as he did in developing his investing world view—even naming his foundation the Open Society Institute. As he explained in the published conversations with Wien and Koenen:

> In my philosophy, open society is based on the recognition that we all act on the basis of imperfect understanding. Nobody is in possession of the ultimate truth. Therefore, we need a critical mode of thinking; we need institutions and rules that allow people with different opinions and interests to live together in peace; we need a democratic form of government that ensures the orderly transfer of power; we need a market economy that provides feedback and allows mistakes to be corrected; we need to protect minorities and respect minority opinions. Above all, we need the rule of law.[25]

His first foray into "open society" investing was in South Africa in 1979, funding university scholarships for promising black youths, but he ended it when he discovered that the university was siphoning off a substantial share of the funds for general purposes.

The early 1980s was a period of extreme tensions in the Cold War, and dissident movements, many of them Jewish, were growing in prominence. The dissident agenda matched up well with Soros's aspirations to assist in the spread of open societies, while his eastern European background combined with his great wealth made him a real-life model of a world freed from the repressive hand of the apparatchiks.

It was also a time of opportunity. In return for long sought recognition of their post–World War II national borders, the Soviet Union and its Eastern European satellites signed the Helsinki Accords in 1975, which included human rights standards among its provisions. That led to the establishment in New York of Helsinki Watch, an organization to track Soviet compliance with the agreement. Soros began to attend the regular meetings of Helsinki Watch, becoming a major supporter of the organization as it expanded its geographical reach worldwide and became Human Rights Watch. Aryeh Neier, the founding director of Helsinki Watch, eventually became the president of Soros's Open Society Institute.

The ability to write a check on the spot is a great advantage for a philanthropist. Soros once shocked his hosts in Hungary, who had been cadging thousand-dollar subventions from western rights groups, by offering them $1 million—and not as an endowment, as they first assumed, but as an annual allowance. By the mid-1980s he was funneling money to rights movements and dissident groups throughout the eastern bloc, including the Polish solidarity movement. One of his greatest successes was in Hungary, where he flooded the universities with modern copiers, breaking the state's monopoly on copying services—which included monitoring exactly who was copying exactly what.[26]

His greatest failure may have been in the former Soviet Union. He spent hundreds of millions, at one point single-handedly supporting the cream of Soviet science during the turmoil that followed the collapse of the Party. All those efforts, like his investments, became swallowed up in the wars of the oligarchs. A string of grassroots Soros-funded Russian foundations managed to survive the 1990s in decent shape, but all were subsequently shut down as Putin began to pull the nation back toward its tsarist, if not quite Stalinist, traditions.

Remarkably, all this activity took place when the foundation had almost no staff. Soros did the traveling and made the policy decisions, much as he was doing for his funds. This was also the same period that he was engaged in the strenuous investing activities documented in his *Alchemy*. Essentially the only staff person through most of that decade was his second wife, Susan, who made sense of the trail of commitments that might follow in the wake of one of George's global swings.

All failures admitted, by the standards of philanthropy, OSI has been a signal success. It's now very big, with a $6 billion endowment as of year-end 2007, all of it from Soros and with a very large payout ratio—usually more than $400 million annually.[27] Its growth has been facilitated by Soros's engrained skepticism of "big concepts," and the importance he assigns to competitive ideas. Instead of operating as a univocal global headquarters, on the model of a Ford or Rockefeller Foundation, there are quasi-independent Open Society foundations, or presences, in sixty countries. While there are multiple program themes—justice, open media, women's rights, education advancement, property rights (through home ownership programs and the like), infectious diseases—they are bound together less by programming than by commitment to the values Soros listed in his conversations with Wien and Koenen.

SOROS ON REGULATION

Soros believes strongly in free markets and free trade, but he also believes that there are special characteristics of *financial* markets that make them especially susceptible to bubbles. Products like oil that are used in production processes have firm tethers on their potential value. (There may have been a bubble in oil markets in 2008, but it was over in just months.) The valuation of financial instruments, by contrast, are restricted only by the imagination of market-makers. The word "credit" comes from the Latin word for "belief." If financiers believe that assets are worth financing, their prices will rise, and they can be used to collateralize more security purchases in a self-amplifying cycle. Rising confidence leads to easier credit standards and higher leverage, increasing upward price momentum. Academic research has recently emphasized the marked "pro-cyclicality" of financial markets, which is part of what Soros embraces under his concept of reflexivity.*

The recent credit crunch, in Soros's view, is the end of a sixty-year superbubble in credit creation.[28] Global debt is now about four times global GDP, while the notional values of outstanding derivatives are at least twice as large as total debt. (Financial instruments are claims on real goods, whereas derivatives are typically claims on financial instruments.) The ratios for the United States, which accounts for a great part of world debt, are even higher.

Soros points to three underlying causes for the credit boom. The first, which dates from the 1930s, is the implied commitment of central banks to absorb the bad loans of their member banks. That implied "put" to the government is a classic moral hazard

---

* The recent credit bubble contains many examples of pro-cyclicality. For example, while commercial banks usually maintain a constant leverage ratio over a boom-and-bust cycle, leverage at the "shadow banks"—broker-dealers, private equity and hedge funds, etc.—that dominated recent lending tends to increase on the way up and contract on the way down, adding to the overshoot in both directions.

that encourages imprudent lending. The second two underlying causes are of more recent vintage. The expansion of trade and globalization of financial markets, and the willingness of developing nations to hold very large dollar reserves, have allowed the United States to run very large international account deficits. (Soros finds it "disgraceful" that the world's richest country is the biggest borrower.) The third underlying cause is the virtual abdication of American financial regulators since 1980.

He admits that there is no backing away from the implied put of bad assets to the government: "Let's face it: When the financial system is endangered, the authorities must cave in. . . . [So] institutions engaged in credit creation must accept the fact that they are being protected by the authorities. They must, therefore, pay a price for it"[29]—which means much tighter control over leverage and asset quality and lower profits and bonuses.

Soros's recommendations for domestic financial regulation could be implemented with little in the way of new laws. Keep a tight control on leverage, especially at the commercial banks, and ensure that all exposures are on balance sheet. Most especially don't allow banks to take exposures with instruments that their senior managers don't understand, which might include a large share of the financial innovations of the past couple of decades. In Soros's words:

> When I say this I speak against my own personal interests and predilections. I am a man of the markets, and I abhor bureaucratic restrictions. I try to find my way around them. For instance, I limit the number of funds I advise so I do not have to register with the Securities and Exchange Commission. But I do believe that financial markets are inherently

unstable; I also recognize that regulations are inherently flawed: Therefore stability ultimately depends on a cat-and-mouse game between markets and regulators. Given the ineptitude of regulators, there is some merit in narrowing the scope and slowing down the rate of financial innovations.[30]

Many of the most recent failures of regulation he attributes to the insistence that markets are subject to scientific laws. "The flaw in monetarism," he said, "is the belief that if you regulate money, you've also regulated credit. It's not true. The willingness to engage in leverage or to deleverage is a separate variable. You have to think about money and the instruments of credit separately." The dot-com bubble, he said, was a "share bubble." Authorities should have intervened by slowing the issuance of new shares, he believes, which the SEC could easily have done. Prior to the advent of efficient-markets theory, he said, the authorities would circularize the banks to cut back on construction loans or tighten consumer credit. "They were often wrong, but they knew they might be wrong, and if it didn't work out they would change it. I think it worked better." The uptick rule for short selling, he says, is a good example of an "irrational rational rule. It might not be logical, but it worked. They should bring it back."[31]

RECOMMENDATIONS FOR THE OBAMA ADMINISTRATION

Soros recently developed a set of detailed proposals for expediting recovery from the current recession. There are five proposals, one of which is directed toward energy policy. A year ago, most people would have considered them quite radical, but now they are well within what might be called the activist mainstream. The summary below is mine, drawn from an advance copy of Soros's *The Crash of 2008 and What It Means*, an updating of his earlier work, *The New Paradigm for Financial Markets* (2008).

There are five elements in his reform program:

1. A fiscal stimulus
2. An overhaul of the residential mortgage system
3. Recapitalization of the banks
4. A new energy policy
5. Reform of the international financial system

Stimulus The stimulus program was already underway as he was writing *The Crash of 2008*. Clearly, Soros considers the fact of a stimulus more important than the specifics. No stimulus can do more than moderate the downturn, but the sooner the money is flowing, the better.

Home mortgages An essential element of home-mortgage reform, in Soros's view, would be to require that the originator bears the risk of credit loss. His favorite model is the Danish system in which mortgage originators can securitize mortgages by creating mortgage bonds, but must replace defaulting mortgages in the collateral pool. (By selling the bonds, the bank is monetizing the future stream of interest payments, and transferring interest rate risk, but not credit risk, to the bond buyer.) The Danish system is sufficiently well established that it functions smoothly without government support. A nice feature is that a homeowner can retire a mortgage by replacing it with an equivalent mortgage bond.*

As an interim step toward such a system, Soros proposes that Fannie Mae and Freddie Mac adopt a Danish-like mortgage contract, and use it for both new mortgages and to refinance existing ones, on uniform and standard terms. Soros envisions that once the private mortgage market has been reestablished (and under suitable regulation), Fannie and Freddie, or a replacement government agency, would withdraw to the role of insurer. Over time, he expects, the need for insurance could be eliminated in several steps, much as it has been in Denmark. In his view, the government could implement his program without legislation.

Recapitalizing banks Soros does not present as detailed a plan here as he does for mortgage finance. He regards the present downturn to be potentially as serious as the Great Depression, and believes the banking system requires substantially more pervasive oversight and regulation. At the same time, however, he hopes that banks will not be put into the same "straitjacket" as they were after the Depression.

He believes that any entity with credit creation powers must be regulated. Variable margin, minimum capital requirements, and central bank directives on channeling credit are once-favored policy

---

* If interest rates rise, both bond prices and home prices fall. In the United States, the result is that homeowners are often locked into their current homes. But a Danish homeowner can take advantage of the fall in prices to discharge her mortgage by buying an equivalent bond at the depressed market price and substituting it for the original mortgage. The position of the bondholders is unaffected.

tools that he'd like to see restored. All financial instruments must be licensed and supervised to ensure that they are transparent and safe. Leverage rules must provide for adequate margins of safety. The overblown, far-too-profitable behemoth institutions that have dominated markets over the past decade must be shrunk, and regulators must work together toward a gradual transition to transnational regulatory oversight.

For the immediate future, the key policy challenge will be "to offset the collapse of credit by creating money, writing off bad debt, and recapitalizing the banks. Then, if and when that succeeds, the excess money supply will have to be drained off as fast as credit begins to flow"—which he concedes will be an extraordinary challenge.

He proposes that the Treasury secretary oversee a valuation of troubled assets according to uniform guidelines. As a bank is valued, and is presumably found to be inadequately capitalized, that same audit will be used to price an equity offering, which will be offered first to the private sector, with any unsold issuances taken up by the Treasury. After the recap, he suggests, the troubled assets will be placed in a "sidepocket" of the bank, capitalized to the value established by the audit, with no further adjustments over their life. From that point, the bank can resume business on normal commercial terms. Soros also suggests that once the recap is completed, minimum capital requirements could be temporarily lowered as an additional stimulus to lending—which would also help offset the projected withdrawal of the government's excess monetary stimulus. His plan would also require that both shareholders and bondholders lose their stakes before government rescue money is available. (Bondholders have been largely protected in the current round of bailouts.)

Energy policy Soros calls for both a carbon tax (or cap and trade system) and a tax on imported oil to put a floor under carbon-based energy prices. The disincentives to carbon-based sources would be matched by substantial investment in conservation, renewables, and alternative sources.

International financial reform Soros worries that the financial chaos that originated in the United States will wreak maximum damage on the newly emerging "periphery" economies. The institution established for crisis finance in international crises, the International Monetary Fund, is short of funds itself, largely because of the Bush administration's bias against internationalist agencies.

He calls for:

1. Combined action by the wealthier countries to donate their special drawing rights (SDR) facilities to a reserve fund that may be drawn upon by poorer countries in order to expand the international money supply.
2. Beefing up the current, small IMF short-term lending facility (STL) by expanding the current quota limits, and through monetary contributions from the wealthier countries.
3. A menu of actions to facilitate access to capital markets by the periphery countries, including guarantees by the wealthier countries of periphery-country bond issues, expansion of currency swap lines, and more.

4. Urgent international steps to unify regulation, coordinate macroeconomic policies, and stabilize commodity price fluctuations.

His closing comment is: "It remains to be seen whether any of the
ideas laid out here are adopted as policy." That phrase betrays a
resigned expectation that they are likely not to be.

NOTE ON CREDIT DEFAULT SWAPS

Soros has strong views on the regulation of credit default swaps,
or CDSs, one of the most important—and most controversial—
recent financial innovations that he regards as "toxic securities." I
am presenting his views in this separate note in order to present
sufficient background for the instruments and for Soros's reasoning,
without breaking the narrative of the chapter.

CDSs are usually thought of as a form of insurance for financial
instruments. The volume of instruments covered by CDSs ballooned from about $1 trillion at the turn of the century to $65
trillion by 2007. Since then, an industry-organized effort to close
out offsetting swaps has lowered the notional values by about half,
to $30-plus trillion. Some recent spectacular losses, like those that
triggered the collapse of the insurance giant AIG, have been related
to credit default swaps.

CDSs originated as a portfolio management tool for banks.
Suppose "U.S. Bank" decides it is underexposed to credits in
Southeast Asia. The old way to fix that was to buy some Asian
bank branches or partner with a local bank. A CDS can short-
circuit the process. For a fee, U.S. Bank will guarantee against
any losses on a loan portfolio held by "Asia Bank," and will receive

the interest and fees on those loans. Asia Bank will continue to service the loans, so its local customers will see no change, but Asia Bank, in street jargon, will have purchased "insurance" for its risk portfolio, freeing up regulatory capital for business expansion.

It was an easy step for large holders of bonds and other debt instruments to use CDSs to protect themselves against losses. The manager of a pension fund with a large mortgage portfolio could purchase default insurance in the form of a CDS, usually with a bank or an insurance company as a counterparty. The attraction for the seller is that it would receive fees with very little capital investment. Sellers usually have to post collateral against their insurance obligation, but major dealer banks and some other highly-rated financial companies are usually exempted from collateral requirements. Collateral requirements were often spottily managed, or even waived, for other players, although by all reports, enforcement has improved considerably over the past couple of years. Before the credit collapse in 2007, bondholders often found that they could buy protection on their bonds for less than their yield, creating "negative carry," or earning positive yields while assuming no risk.

But the main reason CDS volumes exploded is that they are a useful proxy for buying and selling bonds. Selling protection on a corporate bond means that you assume the default risk of the bond and collect fees that approximate its yield—so you are in much the same position as if you had bought the bond, except that you've laid out much less cash. Conversely, buying protection allows you to short bonds, much like buying a stock market put option (the right to sell stock at a specific price). If the price of the bond falls, as the trader anticipates it will, the value of his CDS will rise.

But criticisms of CDSs abound, and with good reason. For one, CDSs are traded "over the counter," rather than through a formal exchange. Although processes are improving, deals are cut individually by the parties, so deal terms and the quality of the paperwork and audit trails vary substantially, which could greatly complicate the effects of market disruption. Work is underway to move CDS to exchanges, but it is proceeding slowly, and some of the more popular forms may not be suitable for technical reasons.

CDSs, moreover, amplify invisible leverage. Assume a firm writes a CDS protecting a $100 million loan portfolio, and posts the full $10 million collateral indicated by current market spreads. The position is effectively the same as buying the bond with 10:1 leverage. But that leverage won't appear on the balance sheet. The great boom in CDSs wasn't so much about buying and selling protection; it happened because CDSs created a highly leveraged, fairly liquid trading environment for bonds and loans. One reason recent bank writeoffs have been shockingly large was that most of the bigger banks' balances contained vast amounts of invisible leverage enabled by innovations like CDSs.

Even more worrisome, the CDS market boomed when bond defaults were at historic lows. Protection was sold against some very smoky stuff, like structured bonds backed by subprime mortgages. While the big CDS dealer banks minimize their risks by balancing their long and short positions, there are rumors of market players, especially hedge funds, that are big net protection sellers. The failure of AIG was triggered by its large losses on "naked" or unhedged protection selling. Even assuming much stricter collateral enforcement, widespread bond failures could conceivably trigger widespread CDS defaults, which would be devastating.

Soros, however, raises a further point that convinces him of the toxicity of CDSs. In all securities markets, there are asymmetries between being short and long. If you sell a stock short (i.e., sell shares that you don't own), you win if the stock falls, but your total winnings can't exceed the sale price (stock prices can't fall past zero). If you lose, on the other hand, because the stock's price rises before you cover the short, your losses, in theory, are potentially infinite. That asymmetry reverses when you are long stocks. Your losses can't be greater than your investment, but in principle, there is no limit on your possible winnings. In general, therefore, the asymmetry of the payoffs between the longs and the shorts favors the longs—which tends to adduce to market stability.

The asymmetries are reversed for CDSs. The short player, or the buyer of protection, has the bigger potential payoff. The most she can lose are her fees, but if a bond defaults, she can collect up to the entire par value of the bond. The long player, the protection seller, however, will collect only the fee revenues over the life of the swap, but faces potentially catastrophic losses when bonds default. Whenever the asymmetries favor the short player, Soros argues, they create market instability since there will be more shorts than longs. "CDSs are a natural bear market instrument," he says.

Moving CDSs to exchanges won't solve the problem, he argues. "I think they should be banned," except for cases where the protection buyer actually owns the bonds he is insuring.[32]

BUFFETT

The year 1984 was the fiftieth anniversary of the publication of what is possibly the most famous investment text in the world: *Security Analysis* by Benjamin Graham and David Dodd. Since the book was written while the authors were teaching at Columbia, the university celebrated the occasion by sponsoring a symposium pitting Warren Buffett, the best-known exponent of Graham-Dodd theory, against Michael Jensen, then at the University of Rochester and a leading advocate of the Chicago School theories of efficient capital markets.

Graham, the senior figure in the Graham-Dodd pairing, is known as the "the father of modern security analysis." He had been a Wall Street wunderkind in the 1920s, before seeing his firm nearly wiped out by the Great Crash. *Security Analysis* was an attempt to draw principles from that experience. Graham mocked the empty investment slogans that passed for wisdom before 1929— like, "Pick out those individual companies which are most likely to grow rapidly."[1] Instead he preached a rigorous analysis of what was most knowable about a security—the company's expected earnings and the expected interest/dividends over a relatively near term, its tangible assets, and their relation to the security's price. You were buying a *company*, he insisted, not just a piece of paper. The wise investor, moreover, always left a good "margin of safety"[2] between her judgment of the company's value and the price she was willing to pay.

Chicago School theorists, by contrast, teach that stock prices always incorporate all available information on all shares, so no single individual can outsmart the market. Outsized investment returns are therefore likely to be based either on luck or inside information. Chicago School theories helped drive the shift toward index-based investing, as well as highly mathematized techniques for managing large investment portfolios.

Buffett opened his talk with a thought experiment.[3] Assume all 225 million people in the United States engaged in a coin-flipping contest, betting $1 they could call the coin. Since all the outcomes are random, the math says that after ten flips, there will be about 220,000 people still in the contest, each with more than $1,000 in winnings (all of them, Buffett said, bragging about the "marvelous insights they bring to the field of flipping"). After twenty flips, there will be only about 215 people still in the contest, each with more than $1 million (and, Buffett said, doubtless writing "books on *How I Turned a Dollar into a Million* . . . ").

Spoilsport business school professors would quickly point out that orangutans would produce the same result. And they would be right. But, Buffett asked, what if "you found that 40 of them came from a particular zoo in Omaha . . . you would probably go out and ask the zookeeper about what he's feeding them." Cancer is usually assumed to be randomly distributed, he went on, but if epidemiologists find a concentration in some little town, good science dictates that "you would get very interested in the water there, or the occupation of those afflicted." Without knowing the causes, "you would know where to search."

Then he laid out the records of nine investment funds, all run by people known to him for many years, and all of whom followed the Graham playbook—from the same zoo, as it were. The table below shows both the general partners' and limited partners' returns compared to the Standard and Poor's 500 Index or the Dow Jones Industrial Average over the measured time period for each fund. (Two cases are not shown; they were pension funds, with results expressed only by high rankings in the pension-fund return universe.)

COMPOUNDED GAINS; ENTIRE PERIOD (PERCENTAGES)

FUND	PERIOD	S&P 500	GP	MULTIPLE GP/S&P	LP	MULTIPLE LP/S&P
No. 1	28 years	887	23,105	26.0	6,679	7.5
No. 2	16 years	239	1,661	6.9	936	3.9
No. 3	12 years*	153	2,795	18.3	1,593	10.4
No. 4	13 years	270	Not reported	Not reported	775	2.9
No. 5	13 years	97	1,156	11.9	500	5.2
No. 6	19 years	306	22,200	72.5	5,530	18.1
No. 7	18 years*	389	4,277	11.0	2,309	5.9

* Benchmark is DJIA.

The orangutans in this zoo, in other words, got *far* better results than the rest of the coin flippers. Cumulative general partner returns were in a range of 7 to 72 times better than the indices, while the LPs did 3 to 18 times better. The uniformly good results, Buffett stressed, were not because they were all making the same investments. In fact, few of them owned the same stocks and their strategies and sectoral concentrations differed considerably. Some, like Buffett, held a relatively small number of companies and were long-term holders, while others had much broader holdings and were active traders.

Nor was the sample "cooked" in any way. Buffett didn't search through the universe of value investors to find the lucky orangutans. These managers, for the most part, had received their early investing indoctrination from Graham or one of his close disciples; they had stayed in touch over the years; and they all followed, more or less, Graham's value-analytic disciplines. The results, he thought, spoke for themselves, and he marveled that business schools were so adamantly uninterested in them.

The rest of the talk was vintage Buffett.

On the extensive econometric studies of stock movements: "It isn't necessarily because such studies have any utility; it's simply that the data are there and academicians have worked hard to learn the mathematical skills needed to manipulate them. Once these skills are acquired, it seems sinful not to use them, even if the usage has no utility or negative utility."

On the illogic of stock timing: "[W]hen businessmen buy businesses . . . I doubt that many are cranking into their purchase decision the day of the week or the month in which the transaction is going to occur. . . . I am baffled why academicians invest extensive time and effort to see whether it makes a difference when buying small pieces of those same businesses."

On risk and reward: "If you buy a dollar bill for 60 cents, it's riskier than if you buy a dollar bill for 40 cents. . . . The Washington Post Company in 1973 was selling for $80 million in the market. [But a fair value of its assets was] not less than $400 million. . . . Now, if the stock had declined even further to . . . $40 million instead of $80 million, its beta [volatility] would have been greater. And to people that think beta measures risk, the cheaper price would have made it look riskier.* This is truly *Alice in Wonderland*."

When Buffett finished, the students gave him a standing ovation. It was, in a way, symbolic. Buffett was just then on the cusp of becoming a financial demigod, the "Sage of Omaha," flashing his homespun barbs at finance professors. More important, he had just become a billionaire.

THE NERDY ROAD TO WEALTH

Warren Buffett was born in Omaha about ten months after the great stock market crash of 1929, the second of three children, and the only boy.[4] His father, Howard, was an insurance man who'd become a stockbroker with a local bank, and duly became

---

* "Beta" is the measure of a stock's average price volatility. "Low beta" stocks, since their prices are more predictable, are considered to be lower-risk investments than stocks with a high beta. Buffett's gibe nicely captures the difference in perspective between an investor prospecting for the best-priced company shares on offer and, say, a pension fund manager attempting to construct an asset *portfolio* to match a projected stream of future liabilities. Investing simply to "beat the market," especially since relatively few managers did it well, often led to pension or endowment portfolios grossly mismatched to the obligations they were intended to finance. Chicago School efficient-markets theories were one of a number of useful assumptions that refocused managers' attention from stock picking to longer-term portfolio management issues. Useful and intellectually interesting hypotheses, however, have a way of hardening into dogma, especially in academia, and especially when they can't be rigorously tested.

unemployed when the bank shut down in 1931. But Howard was tenacious, as his son would be. He opened his own stock brokerage and actually made a good living during the 1930s, eventually serving four terms in Congress as a rock-ribbed antilabor Republican.

Warren was an unusual child: very bright, but socially awkward and immature well into adulthood; not good at team sports, but a fierce ping-pong player; a loner, but with the drive to dragoon friends and acquaintances into working on his multiple enterprises. Business and money were an obsession from an early age—not obsessive in a miserly sense, but in the way of the dedicated art collector or video game addict. By age six, he was selling gum and Coca-Cola door to door. In elementary school, he was running adult-scale newspaper routes. When he was twelve, one of his father's business acquaintances asked Warren to sell off the excess stocks of a failing warehouse operation. What's striking about the episode isn't that Warren handled the sale smoothly, which he did, but that the businessman made the proposal to Warren directly—man-to-man as it were—without first asking his father. During his high school years, his businesses included a pinball machine franchising operation, a used golf-ball business, publishing a racetrack tout sheet, and a forty-acre tenant farm, which he had purchased for $1,200. Warren finished high school with a $5,000 savings account, equivalent to about $53,000 in today's money.

The Buffett brain was an almost perfectly evolved money-processing organism. His near-photographic recall of voluminous amounts of financial material—textbooks, *Moody's* reports, company finances—and his fascination with numbers have a vaguely autistic aura. As a kid, he kept notebooks full of passing license plates, memorized city population numbers, counted occurrences of letters in texts, and, at age eleven, was almost transported by the discovery of interest compounding in a book called *One Thousand Ways to Make $1,000.*

After high school, Warren went to Wharton, then an undergraduate business school at the University of Pennsylvania. At Wharton, he distinguished himself by his social clumsiness and his obnoxiousness in class—after the first week or so, he knew all the business textbooks by heart and liked to correct professors who misquoted their own books. Unhappy in Philadelphia, he finished up at the University of Nebraska. Failing to get into Harvard Business School, he went to Columbia, took Graham's class, and found his vocation.

Graham quickly recognized Buffett's great talents in stock valuation. He had inhaled every case and every example from the Graham-Dodd tome, and could talk perceptively about almost any stock in the market. He was the only student in the securities class to get an A+, and Graham freely gave him high job recommendations. Buffett's dream was to get hired at Graham's investment firm, Graham-Newman, but Graham gently explained that very few firms on Wall Street hired Jews, so he reserved his own small number of job openings for his co-religionists.

Buffett returned to Omaha to an unhappy stint in his father's brokerage. While he felt at home in Omaha above all places on earth, he hated brokerage. For one thing, at age twenty-one (and looking and acting even younger), older people were reluctant to take his advice. Then he always felt awful when someone bought a stock on his recommendation and it went down. And finally, he didn't like the implicit conflict of interest in stock brokerage. Successful stock salesmen focused on the sale, not the stock, and made the most money by churning customer accounts, constantly selling and buying. Buffett felt much more comfortable investing for himself.

Despite his misgivings, within a year or so, he was doing very well. He was building a client base, especially from people who knew him from graduate school. An article he wrote on his favorite stock, GEICO, the first direct-mail insurer, drew a job offer from one of the heirs to the Sears, Roebuck fortune, but National Guard duties kept him at home. He taught an adult evening course on investing at the University of Omaha. The students loved throwing the names of stocks at him. Buffett had read, and substantially committed to memory, all 10,000 pages of the *Moody's Manuals*—financial analyses of virtually every traded company—and he could speak impromptu, and in depth, about almost any of them. He was working on his social skills, conscientiously applying the rules in Dale Carnegie's *How to Win Friends and Influence People*, and attending Dale Carnegie school classes. On top of that, nerdy and socially awkward Warren had fallen in love with a popular and vivacious young woman, Susie Thompson, the daughter of a dean at the university. After a tenacious courtship, against all odds, they married in 1952.

And then in 1954, finally, he got an offer from Graham-Newman. He had stayed in touch in the years since his graduation, exchanging letters on stock recommendations, and taking any excuse for a trip to New York so he could drop in and visit Graham. There was no question but that he would he accept the offer. So Warren and Susie, with baby Susie in tow and a second child on the way, moved to a small apartment in White Plains. Although Buffett was affluent by 1950s standards—he'd finished Columbia with a portfolio worth almost $20,000, and had far more than that by the time his family moved to New York—the couple lived very frugally. (Buffett always measured the price of a new purchase against the future value of the same dollars at his normal rate of compounding.) During his first few weeks on the job, he sat in the company file room, and read every page in every file.

Two deals at Graham-Newman were important learning experiences, and typify the Buffett thought process. The first involved a candy company in Brooklyn that had just been taken over by Jay Pritzker, of the Chicago real estate family, who later built the Hyatt hotel chain. Pritzker was closing down an unprofitable product line and wanted to reduce his inventory of cocoa beans. Instead of simply selling them on the open market, he decided to exchange them for shares to increase his ownership percentage. He offered shareholders a stock buyback deal, in which they could turn in a share of stock, then worth $34, for a tradable warehouse certificate for a bag of cocoa beans worth $36. Ben Graham loved that kind of deal, and he assigned Buffett to execute the trades (which also entailed locking in the cocoa bean price in the futures market).

Applying his usual microscope, Buffett calculated that Pritzker had disproportionately allocated his cocoa bean inventory among outsiders' shares and those he was retaining, a disproportion that would only grow as shares were retired. Unless there was a major break in cocoa prices, the intrinsic per-share value of the company should rise. The presence of so well-known a name as Pritzker as the controlling investor would also inevitably draw attention to the stock. So while Buffett diligently booked the $2 a share arbitrage profit for Graham-Newman, he bought and retained stock for his own account, soon selling out at $2\frac{1}{2}$ times his investment.

The second deal was an obscure Massachusetts bus company, which had built up huge cash reserves—about $60 a share, while the stock was selling in the $30 to $35 range. The management was buying back shares, both reducing their cash and increasing the share value. Buffett started competitive share buying on his own hook, taking out ads in the local papers, and contacting the bigger shareholders directly from the lists maintained by the state public utility regulators. Then, with his usual absolute self-confidence on financial matters, he drove to Massachusetts to meet the company president—and learned that the company was considering a special dividend to reduce its cash hoard, possibly as much as $50. Buffett never knew whether the dividend was in reaction to his buying campaign. He hadn't put any direct pressure on the company, and treated the visit as a friendly fact-finding expedition. But his buying forays would have been a warning signal of the feeding frenzy that might ensue as more professionals learned of the share mispricing. Buffett kept buying, of course, and within weeks booked a $20,000 profit.

Buffett quickly became the young star of Graham-Newman, along the way making friends with like-thinking young men he would work with for much of his life. They included Walter Schloss, a young assistant at Graham-Newman when Buffett came to the firm, who later had left to start investing on his own, and Tom Knapp and Bill Ruane, who worked at other firms but were part of the Graham coterie. These three eventually managed funds that Buffett used as examples in his Columbia presentation. Another useful contact was Henry Brandt, a young stockbroker who later made a career working almost exclusively as an investment source for Buffett.

Much as he enjoyed the work, Buffett decided to leave in 1956, when he learned that Graham was retiring. He was offered a partnership in a successor firm with Newman's son, but he decided to return to Omaha. It was apparently an easy decision. The commute from White Plains was taxing, he was homesick for Omaha, and the whole point in going east was to work under Ben Graham. The Buffetts arrived back home just as Warren was turning twenty-six. He didn't have a job but wasn't planning to get one. In today's dollars, he was already a millionaire.

The short time at Graham-Newman sheds an interesting light on Buffett's lifelong adulation of Graham, and his eager assumption of the Graham-Dodd mantle. In truth, he was never a classic Graham-Dodd investor. Buffett was still a Graham graduate student when he bought one of the first of his favorite companies, GEICO—which today remains a core property in the Buffett portfolio. But at the time, GEICO didn't fit the Graham investing model. Originally the Government Employees Insurance Company, GEICO was founded in 1936 by two entrepreneurs, Leo Goodwin and Cleves Rhea, who spotted a massive cost-saving and price-shaving opportunity in direct marketing of standardized insurance policies to prime market groups, without commissioned insurance agents. (Government employees, they reasoned, led more careful lives than the general population.) Years later, when the Rhea family negotiated a block sale of their holdings to institutional investors, Graham-Newman snapped up a major stake, and Graham was installed as chairman.

Buffett learned about the company from Graham. Wanting to learn everything about his idol, he called on the company, pushed into the office of a senior executive, introduced himself as Graham's student, and had a long conversation about the company. (The executive was equally fascinated by Buffett and his deep grasp of insurance.) Buffett loved GEICO's low costs, the rapid growth, and the fact that insurance companies generated investable cash well before any claims were paid. He immediately sold most of his stock portfolio and invested in GEICO. But GEICO's steady appreciation after the original Graham purchase, on bargain terms, placed it well out of the usual Graham-Dodd "value stock" range. Its price-to-earnings multiple was still lower than the industry average, but it was a very small company in a field dominated by giants. Buffett was buying a compelling growth story, which is the opposite of value-investing logic.

Similarly with his cocoa bean deal. The cautious Graham was happy picking up the $2 per-share arbitrage earnings. Buffett's stock purchase strategy involved a big bet on cocoa bean prices. Yes, retiring outsider shares swelled the asset-value-to-share-price ratio, but prices of commodities like cocoa beans can be very volatile, so he was taking on substantial risk.

Nor would Graham have approved of his visit to the Massachusetts bus company. Graham attended board meetings, but he thought of shareholders and management as opposing sides. Fraternizing with the enemy, as it were, could compromise one's independent judgment. Finally, Graham preached extreme diversification, and he would have been horrified at Buffett putting the lion's share of his wealth into a single stock like GEICO, a growth stock to boot.

Buffett's investment style, in short, does not fit a mold. His success is grounded in a unique talent set: the rare ability to size up managements and companies, and the capacity to gather and synthesize prodigious amounts of information and then laser in on a business's heart. His investment style is the polar opposite of George Soros's, but they both have a quality of genius that can't be captured in a textbook.

GOING IT ALONE

Buffett's objective, when the family settled back in Omaha, was to become a millionaire by investing for his own account. With about $175,000 in capital, it was a realistic goal. But he wanted to do it fast, and that meant getting more money to manage, which he raised from friends and family—a very dangerous proposition. Susie's father put in $25,000, his life savings. An aunt put up $35,000. His roommate at Wharton, who thought Buffett was a hick but was dazzled by his financial acumen, put up $5,000 of his own money and $25,000 that belonged to his mother. Buffett's sister and her husband put in $10,000. None of these people was poor—in the mid-1950s, $25,000 was a *lot* of money—but they were at best upper-middle class. It's easy to imagine the tension on the Buffett marriage if Warren had lost all of Susie's father's savings. But he seems to have had no doubts. As he told his biographer, Alice Schroeder, "These were the people who believed in me. There's no way in the world I would have taken my aunt Alice's or my sister's or my father-in-law's money if I had thought that I'd lose it. At point I didn't think I could lose money over time."[5]

The terms of his first partnership were both unusually fair and unusually strict. Buffett did not charge asset-based management fees; the first 4 percent of earnings belonged entirely to the investors, while half of anything over that went to Buffett. Most unusually, Buffett took a quarter of any losses, without limitation. The trade-off for the generous investment terms was that he provided only the barest minimum of information on the portfolio, a rule that he maintained for many years with all investors. He reported no specifics at all about individual investments. (The thought of worried investor calls during a market downturn made him almost ill.) Instead, he released an annual report on overall performance and fee splits; at the time of the report, there would be a brief window for partners to withdraw their capital, if any were so minded. Buffett's own investment in the partnership was only $100. His own money—which was more than the partnership's—he managed separately with the goal of providing $12,000 a year for living expenses.

The first year of the partnership, the cash return was $4,500, or more than 7 percent annualized. (The arrangement began in May.) The S&P 500 did about 3 percent that same year. Net of the Buffett fee split, therefore, the partners got 5 $1/2$ percent—not knock-your-socks-off, but respectable. Buffett's share was 1 $1/2$ percent, which he left in the partnership, as he continued to do for many years.

And the client base grew. In September 1956, Graham referred one of his former clients, who visited Omaha during a cross-country trip, spent a while talking to Buffett, and sent him $120,000. The next year, a well-known New York money manager, whom Buffett had met and impressed while he was at Columbia, recommended him to a prominent Omaha urologist. The doctor and his wife interviewed Buffett and thought he looked like a teenager. But they liked his straightforwardness, his clarity, and the fairness of his terms; they gave him $100,000. Wealthier Omahans had begun to hear about him and invest as well. All this time, Buffett worked out of his home—essentially alone whether family was with him or not—poring over *Moody's* and company annual reports. He kept expenses to the barest minimum, did all the paperwork and bookkeeping himself, carried the growing trove of stock certificates to and from the bank's safe-deposit box—tying up all the little details, even as his brain was alive with visions.

Buffett wanted to raise a lot of money. He had little interest in the passive, highly diversified Graham style, the one his friend Walter Schloss was employing with great success in New York. Buffett preferred to concentrate on fewer companies that he really believed in, and to get a big enough position to have a say when he thought the business was going off track.

Sanborn Map was an early prototype for the evolving Buffett style. It was a boring company, but with an investment portfolio worth some 40 percent more than its stock price. That was attractive, but worth nothing to a shareholder if it was kept locked up in an undervalued company. So Buffett took a big position, investing about a third of his funds under management, and rounding up co-investors from friends and business acquaintances, until his group had accumulated enough shares to elect him to a board seat. He went to a board meeting and discovered that the board was an old-boys' club—mostly insurance executives with minimal Sanborn stock holdings. They thought everything was fine just as it was.

Irritated, Buffett expanded his network, organizing enough share accumulation to gain a control position. After one more eventless meeting, he threatened a special shareholder meeting to unseat the board. The board caved, and submitted to a Pritzker/cocoa-bean type of exchange. The portfolio was equitably allocated among all shareholders, with the right to exchange their shares for their allocations, locking in a very large gain.

It took more than a year to bring Sanborn to heel, and at times it was all-consuming, but it showed another side of Buffett. He always shrank from personal confrontations and hated to fire employees, but if one of his holdings was acting against the interests of its shareholders, he would march right into the trenches, guns blazing.

Word was spreading, even among the most skeptical of Omahans. In four years—through 1960—his investors had realized a 24 percent annual rate of return against the Dow's 9 percent. Buffett's reinvested incentive fees had pushed his share of the fund to nearly a quarter-million dollars. Together with his own portfolio, he was close to becoming a millionaire. It was time to get a proper office, and to get some help with the paperwork. He took space in Kiewit Plaza, the same spot from which he operates today. All the partnerships and his own portfolio were rolled into a single entity, Buffett Partnership Ltd. (BPL).

The reorganization came at a time when markets were breaking in a way that would create a virtual picnic for someone with Buffett's instincts. There was a sharp market correction in 1962. BPL emerged relatively unscathed, with lots of dry powder, while the correction left huge swathes of shares seriously undervalued. This was the time to act on the famous Graham dictum: "Be fearful when others are greedy, and greedy when others are fearful."[6]

An opportunity for constructive greed was duly proffered by American Express. One of its incidental businesses was certifying storage tank receipts in a New Jersey soybean oil tank field. An operator named Tony De Angelis somehow fooled American Express employees into certifying tanks of seawater as containing soybean oil. When a sudden soybean oil price break in the fall of 1963 exposed De Angelis's fraud, American Express was left holding the bag for as much as $175 million in losses. The company's stock went into freefall, amid worries that it could fail.

American Express's primary products, however, were "Traveler's Cheques," and, at the threshold of the plastic era, an elite credit card business. Travelers' checks were a form of safe currency. You bought them at face value and could cash them at an American Express office in almost any sizeable city in the world. Any business whose customers routinely ponied up interest-free cash advances quickened Buffett's pulse, the more so with the post–De Angelis stock price collapse. He had just begun to investigate more closely when John Kennedy was assassinated. The market tanked, and American Express led the plunge into the abyss.

Buffett called Harry Brandt, his New York broker buddy, and asked him to make a field investigation. Brandt spent the next several days loitering in department stores, hanging around hotel checkout counters, visiting travelers' check cash locations. Back came a thick report: Travelers and high-end shoppers were using their American Express checks and credit cards routinely, as a perfectly natural thing to do. No one seemed worried, or even aware, that the stock was in trouble.

Buffett pondered the information, and later reported to his partners that he had a "high-probability insight."[7] He had discovered the very un-Grahamian notion of a "franchise" or "a brand" or the value of "goodwill" in the non-accounting sense of the term. A growing segment of the affluent public considered American Express products to be an intrinsic part of daily transactions. *That* was the asset that really mattered, much more than inventory or cash on the balance sheet. Insights like that, he later told his partners, "is what causes the cash register to really sing." At one point, a third of the portfolio was in American Express. The 1965 partnership per-share gains were a hair short of 24 percent.

The other major deal Buffett made around this time was to buy a midsize New England textile maker named Berkshire Hathaway. It fit all the Graham-Dodd *Securities Analysis* criteria—steady, boring, low price-to-asset ratio. Buffett spent an enormous amount of time and energy trying to make it a success, but the times and production methods were rapidly moving away from the likes of Berkshire Hathaway, although it was years before Buffett conceded that he couldn't make it work. (The price-to-asset ratios so beloved by the Grahamians missed tidal currents like technology shifts.) He gained control of the company in 1965, nine years after returning to Omaha and starting the first family-and-friends partnership. By that time, his total funds under management had passed the $50 million mark, and Buffett's personal net worth was about $9 million.

And he was thinking about a new business model.

THE FIRST BILLION IS THE HARDEST

The Dow broke 1,000 in 1968, and Buffett started unloading his high fliers, like American Express. He guessed a long downturn was coming, and fretted about his limited partners' expectations of spectacular wealth compounding forever. Warren Buffett, of course, loved downturns; they were his richest stalking grounds. But they could also presage an extended period of flat returns for his limiteds. So in 1969, with the Dow already down to 800, he decided to wind up his investment vehicle, BPL.

Buffett naturally kept on investing, focusing on companies that threw off cash to fund more investments, companies like Blue Chip, a trading stamp company—stores bought the stamps, and the company had the use of the money until prizes were redeemed. In the same mold was an Illinois bank and a Nebraska insurance company, both of which Buffett had been tracking for years. (Buffett measured insurance companies by how much he paid for "float"—policyholders' cash held against future payouts—that he could invest. An insurance holding was a success when the float was free.) He also invested, then mostly disinvested, in retail clothing, and began to dabble in publishing—the Omaha *Sun* and a mildly left-of-center start-up, the *Washington Monthly*. Neither had much financial significance, but Buffett greatly enjoyed stage-managing a 1972 *Sun* exposé of the huge cash troves built up at Nebraska's Catholic Boys' Town, of Father Flanagan fame—a reporting coup that won the paper a Pulitzer. Finally, as he soured on the future of Berkshire Hathaway, he began to close down its less profitable divisions and use it as a holding company for the insurance and banking investments.

Nineteen-seventy-two was also the year that George Goodman (writing under the name Adam Smith) published *Supermoney*, a huge best-seller. The book concentrated on the hot new portfolio managers and the new mathematical investing technologies. But Goodman, who sniffed out the dangerous lack of common sense in investing fads, had also spent time with Ben Graham, who had sent him to Warren Buffett. Goodman devoted most of a long chapter to Buffett, and he was the first to paint a portrait of the aw-shucks, unpretentious, homespun philosopher of the plains, beating all the city slickers by a country mile.

By this time, Buffett had also acquired a partner of sorts— Charlie Munger, a California lawyer six years Buffett's senior, with Omaha roots. The two had been introduced in 1959 and bonded instantly, discovering that their thought processes were almost identical. For many years, they operated separately, but stayed in constant contact, frequently investing side by side. Munger brought in the trading stamp deal, for instance. After another reorganization in 1983, Munger became the number two at Berkshire Hathaway, although his holdings never approached Buffett's. From that point on, Buffett's shareholder communications were usually framed as "Charlie and I think—"

As part of the wind-down of BPL, the limited partners learned for the first time what their holdings actually consisted of. After years of glittering returns, the scruffy-looking little portfolio was a bit of an anticlimax. They had a big position in a textile company that Buffett didn't think was worth much on its own, but which had bank and insurance holdings; there was Blue Chip; inside Blue Chip, there was a retail operation that was mostly a shell, holding cash from recent divestments; and finally a scattering of publications of little financial importance. Some of the share holdings, moreover, were unregistered, so they couldn't be sold on stock exchanges.

Buffett gave the limited partners the choice of cashing out at current values or taking their pro rata shares in the companies. If they took the cash, he advised, they might consider investing it in stock index funds or blue-chip bonds. And although he desperately wanted them to take the cash, which would increase his share of the portfolio, he dutifully told them that it was his intention to hold on to the shares, and to buy more if he could. When it was all over, counting the shares that had been turned in, plus those he was still buying, Buffett had more than doubled his share of the companies in the portfolio.

And naturally, Buffett kept on buying: See's Candies, a very profitable California company that Munger championed (which, with their lack of interest in organization charts, they stuck into Blue Chip); and, taking advantage of new networks opened by the *Sun* Pulitzer, more shares in media companies (some housed in Berkshire, some in Blue Chip). Buffett also began to accumulate *Washington Post* stock. At the height of its Watergate investigations, there was a possibly politically motivated regulatory attack on its most profitable television properties, battering its share price. The paper's publisher, Katherine Graham, was alarmed when she learned that Buffett was buying, fearing that he was a corporate raider. Buffett, who by then had acquired a 12 percent stake, simply offered a written pledge not to buy additional shares without her personal approval. (He knew very well that the capital structure made a hostile raid impossible.) Buffett and Graham soon became the closest of friends; he took a seat on the *Post* board and was the first person she turned to for important business advice. For her part, she extended a hand to Buffett socially, attempting to apply a bit of polish, and took him on a guided tour of the inner corridors of power.

The *Post* performed extremely well for Buffett for a long time. But his favorite investment of the 1970s was GEICO, the company he had first fallen in love with when he was still at Columbia. GEICO was the kind of cash machine Buffett loved. At the start of his career, he had invested a large share of his still-limited wealth in the company, but he eventually divested when even juicier opportunities ran across his desk. By the time he was less cash-constrained, GEICO shares had risen well beyond his margin of safety.

GEICO's success was based on low costs, low-priced insurance, and low-risk customers. But in the go-go years of the 1960s, GEICO made a run for growth, selling low-priced insurance to almost all comers. By 1974, it had rocketed to fifth place among auto insurers, with a stock price that peaked at $61. The out-of-control under-writing caught up with it in 1975, when it posted a shocking $190 million loss. The following year, with its stock in single digits, and facing a shutdown threat from its primary regulator in the District of Columbia, the board fired its management team and, in May, brought in Jack Byrne, an experienced insurance turnaround hand.

Byrne was a whirlwind. He reduced staff by about a fifth, shut down operations in states where rates were unprofitable, trimmed and refocused the business lines, and actually turned a small profit by the fourth quarter. The regulators were impressed, but the company needed capital. Buffett was watching carefully, and asked Kay Graham, who knew Byrne, to introduce them. Byrne had never heard of Buffett and wasn't interested. But the elder statesman of GEICO, Lorimer Davidson, a board member and former CEO, was the same GEICO executive who had been so impressed by the young Ben Graham devotee who had shown up in his office twenty-five years earlier to pepper him with questions about in-

surance. Hearing that Byrne had snubbed Buffett, he told him—
there are various versions of the colorful language he used—to get
back to Buffett right away.

The GEICO investment was the first large-scale demonstration
of what became a typical Buffett takeover operation. He first spent
several hours with Byrne, ostensibly asking questions but actually
assessing Byrnes's understanding of the company and the business.
Then he began quietly to accumulate stock, which was bobbing
around at about $2. Buffett helped out by providing some reinsur-
ance (risk insurance for insurance companies) through a reinsurer
in the Berkshire portfolio, and made calls to regulators to tell them
that he was personally putting a lot of cash into GEICO. They
knew he had very deep pockets, so they could cut GEICO some
slack.

Capital was still the primary problem, though. Byrne was making
the rounds of investment banks with little success, until on a
second try, with help from a junior banker, he got a hearing from
Salomon's semi-legendary boss, John Gutfreund. It was a propitious
time. Salomon was a bond shop but was interested in making a
foray into the more lucrative equities business. After a long discussion, Gutfreund agreed to underwrite the whole deal for $76
million. That was very risky for Salomon; like almost all investment
banks at the time, it was a private partnership with limited capital.
To shore up that commitment, Buffett visited Gutfreund and told
him that he would take the entire issue if necessary. Characteristically, he also made Salomon lower the offering price.

The offering sold so well that Buffett managed to take only about
a quarter of it. But he had a board seat in GEICO, the company in
which Ben Graham still had his life savings. Graham, unfortunately,

had died shortly before the deal closed, so he never knew how his estate had benefited from Buffett's intervention. Although Buffett was GEICO's controlling shareholder for many years, he did not acquire all of it until 1995, when it was throwing off billions of low-cost cash to finance a continuing stream of Berkshire acquisitions. The sharp jump in the GEICO stock price after the financing contributed to a blowout 59 percent Buffett investment performance in 1976.

The successes of the early 1970s, however, were considerably dimmed by a far-reaching SEC investigation into Buffett's and Munger's methods. Suspicions eventually focused on the ramshackle structure of the holding companies, which looked purposely obfuscating, as if they were hiding paper trails. The transaction that drew the most attention was the 1973 purchase of a California savings and loan called Wesco.

Wesco was publicly traded but with a controlling block held by the founding family. The last family member on the board, Betty Peters, was chafing at a sleepy management and had begun pushing for a sale or merger. Buffett and Munger saw a very solid operation with good cash flow, low costs, and a cheap stock, so they began acquiring shares. Their plan was derailed with an announcement that Wesco would be acquired by a flashier, fast-growing California S&L that Wall Street loved. Buffett and Munger were skeptical of the high-flier, and thought Wesco was selling too cheaply. They finally convinced Peters, and to the consternation of the board because she had started the merger push, she blocked the sale. Wesco's stock tanked, so Buffett and Munger could have bought it very cheaply. Instead, they offered a price roughly at the high just before the broken merger. They had no obligation to do that, of course, and it was a spectacular departure from their usual tight-fisted ways. But they felt obligated to Peters and wanted her and her shareholders to come out whole. Wesco was lodged in Blue Chip; Charlie ran Blue Chip, although Berkshire was its biggest shareholder, and he had done the heavy lifting on Wesco.

Why, the SEC investigators wondered, would Buffett and Munger, who always paid the lowest price, pay 50 percent more than they had to for an acquisition that was already in the palms of their hands? They suspected some kind of manipulation was taking place. There ensued the kind of all-court investigative press that almost never concludes without a scalp nailed to the door. It went on for months. Buffett and Munger both testified extensively, without the aid of lawyers, explaining how they worked and the informality of their internal arrangements, and they lamely argued that paying a too-high price was just the right thing to do. Buffett was very worried—he was in the midst of discussions with Kay Graham about a seat on the *Post* board, and he was extremely sensitive about his reputation. But as Munger told him, "If a policeman follows you down the road for five hundred miles, you're going to get a ticket."[8]

At the end of the day, the SEC finally bought their story, delivering only the lightest tap on the wrist. Buffett and Munger agreed to rationalize their bramble bush of holding companies, and while neither admitting nor denying anything, they promised that, whatever it was, they would never do it again. Word of the investigation had, of course, leaked out, but the SEC pointedly gave Buffett a de facto seal of approval by appointing him to a blue-ribbon committee two weeks after the investigation was closed.

The long-promised 1983 reorganization finally rolled all the different businesses into a single holding company, Berkshire Hathaway, with Warren Buffett as chairman and Charlie Munger as vice chairman, although Buffett stressed that he and Charlie were co-managers. There were seven main operating businesses: an insurance group; a newspaper, the *Buffalo Evening News;* the Nebraska Furniture Mart; the candy company; Wesco; Precision Steel, a small specialty steelmaker; and a savings and loan (although Precision and the S&L were both owned by Wesco).

The *Buffalo Evening News* was one of the more traumatic of the Berkshire acquisitions. Buffett and Munger had long been searching for a one-newspaper city, the kind of franchise they preferred and that Buffett sometimes referred to as "a toll bridge."[9] Buffalo had two newspapers, but the *News*, the evening paper, was by far the stronger franchise, although its competitor had a Sunday paper. Berkshire bought the *News* for $35 million and immediately started a Sunday paper. The competitor sued on vague antitrust grounds—that an outside group of speculators were coming to town to run the competition out of business and then raise prices. A hometown court ruled for the competitor, and the *News* limped along under judicial restraints for years,* until Buffett was ready to wash his hands of the whole thing. Higher courts reversed the local decision, and the competitor finally closed shop. Buffett and Munger at last had their "toll bridge," but only after facing

---

* The "toll bridge" crack, which Buffett had once made in an interview, was taken as a statement of intent to put the competitor out of business.

down a potentially nasty strike. It was worth it; the *News* produced $27 million in operating profits in 1984, nearly 80 percent of the purchase price.

The Nebraska Furniture Mart was the perfect Buffett business. Goodman tells of his 1969 visit with Buffett in *Supermoney*:

> We are driving down a street in Omaha; and we pass a large furniture store. I have to use letters in the story because I can't remember the numbers. "See that store?" Warren says. "That's a really good business. It has a square feet of floor space, does an annual volume of b, has an inventory of only c, and turns over its capital at d."
>
> "Why don't you buy it?" I said.
>
> "It's privately held," Warren said.
>
> "Oh," I said.
>
> "I might buy it anyway," Warren said. "Someday."[10]

He did, in 1983. The store was run by "Mrs. B," Rose Blumkin, and her family. Mrs. B was ninety-one years old in 1984 and was at the store all day seven days a week. Buffett adored her. He told his shareholders, "Mrs. B . . . probably makes more decisions in a day than most CEOs do in a year (better ones too)." As he described his buyout, "[The business] had never had an audit and we did not request one; we did not take an inventory nor verify the receivables; we did not check property titles. We gave Mrs. B a check for $55 million and she gave us her word. That made for an even exchange."

He went on:

I have been asked by a number of people just what secrets the Blumkins bring to their business. These are not very esoteric. All members of the family: (1) apply themselves with an enthusiasm and energy that would make Ben Franklin and Horatio Alger look like dropouts; (2) define with extraordinary realism their area of special competence and act decisively on all matters within it; (3) ignore even the most enticing propositions falling outside of that area of special competence; and (4) unfailingly behave in a high-grade manner with everyone they deal with. (Mrs. B boils it down to "sell cheap and tell the truth.")[11]

It was a good recipe. The store's operating profits were $14.5 million in 1984, more than a quarter of its purchase price.

The only underperformer was the insurance group. Berkshire's strong balance sheet was a great competitive advantage in insurance, and GEICO continued to churn out a steady stream of cash. The investment performance was also very strong. The non-GEICO companies, though, had big underwriting losses. Recognizing that reinsurance and casualty loss ratios were much harder to forecast than property losses—especially with the trend toward very high jury awards—Buffett was still "embarrassed" by the results. Total casualty losses were $48 million, against investment gains of $68 million. The unit was profitable, that is, but should have been much more so.

Besides the operating businesses, Berkshire Hathaway had a $1.2 billion stock portfolio (purchased for less than $600 million). There were only ten stocks to speak of; the three biggest holdings were Exxon, General Foods, and Time Inc.

Overall, the book value of Berkshire Hathaway was just crossing the $3 billion mark. Buffett owned more than a third of it. He was a billionaire. Even better, he had finally found the man, Ajit Jain, who could fix his insurance group, so the cash machine would thereafter run more or less the way he always thought it should.

. . . AND THE NEXT BILLIONS ARE OFTEN EASIER

Buffett was just a kid when he was entranced by the magic of compounding. An investment of $1,000 compounded at 10 percent a year for 20 years transmutes into more than $6,700. Double the compounding rate to 20 percent, and you get more than $38,000. If you start with billions rather than thousands, and sustain a high compounding rate, you become very rich indeed.

His arrival in the ranks of Forbes's billionaires—Buffett was one of only fourteen in 1985—opened floodgates of new opportunities. The buyout boom, the infamous "Decade of Greed," was at its Gilded Age peak. Almost all companies were in play. Besieged executives began to see Berkshire as a potential port in a storm. Tom Murphy was head of Capital Cities, a chain of broadcasters that he had built into a modest television station empire. He was also a longtime friend of Buffett's who admired his honesty, his work ethic, and his canny skill in acquisition engineering. When the ABC network, struggling through a bad patch, came under threat from hostile raiders, it sought out Murphy as a "White Knight" acquirer. He took the bait, and then asked Buffett for advice on financing it. As he had hoped, Buffett said that he needed a friendly "gorilla" investor big enough to block a raid. And, yes, Buffett was delighted to play that role. Berkshire thereupon took

15 percent of what at that time was the biggest media deal in history—ABC, dozens of television and radio stations, fifty-plus cable
systems, and nearly a hundred publications. Big moves like that
got the attention of heavy hitters, like star banker Jamie Dimon and
publishing tycoon Walter Annenberg, both of whom made a point
of getting to know Warren Buffett. Buffett also benefited from the
other end of the buyout frenzy. Berkshire had a big position in
General Foods, and reaped a $332 million profit when Philip Morris
snapped it up in 1985. By 1987, Buffett was a *two*-billionaire.

Buffett instinctively distrusted the leveraged buyout craze. Shareholder rights were almost a religion with him, much as they were
for Graham. The buyout fund chiefs, in Buffett's view, were engaged in a massive wealth transfer from companies and shareholders
to themselves and their teams.* The selling shareholders might
get a windfall, but the company would be loaded up with debt,
the investors would extract deal and management fees, and remaining shareholders, employees, or subordinate bondholders
would eventually get it in the neck. Buyout firms love to talk about
"building wealth," but financial engineering more often redistributes

---

* Although Buffett's strictures are well justified, they don't really apply to the
earlier phases of the 1980s buyouts. Big American corporations had enjoyed
almost seventy years of global dominance, virtually without foreign competition
(by grace of two global wars that fattened American coffers and destroyed overseas
capacities). And they had, predictably, become bloated, self-contented bureau-
cracies that collapsed at the first assaults by hungry new competitors in the 1970s.
The first few years of the buyouts broke up the old behemoths, a classic episode
of creative destruction. By about 1985, and certainly by 1986, however, it had
turned into a typical Wall Street feeding frenzy. More and more firms plunged
into the market and buyout prices rose to ridiculous heights, until it all blew
apart in 1989 and 1990.

wealth, only coincidentally in productive ways. The giveaway is that financial buyers almost always focus on the "takeout"—the economics of a deal, that is, usually turn on the chance of a subsequent sale through a public stock offering or a corporate acquisition. The emphasis on a quick sale pushes managers toward short-term window dressing, like the paint jobs of house flippers. Buffett believes that you create wealth only by building *companies*, which takes a long-term commitment.

The Buffett approach to buyouts was epitomized by Scott Fetzer, an Ohio conglomerate selling everything from encyclopedias to vacuum cleaners. Buffett, who kept tabs on almost every public company of significance, knew it was profitable and intelligently and conservatively managed. The CEO tried to execute a leveraged buyout that immediately attracted the attention of a noted raider. From the all-seeing aerie in Omaha came a letter, "We don't do unfriendly deals. If you want to pursue a merger, call me." A deal was struck at $410 million in cash, as Buffett preferred. The scale of the Scott Fetzer deal, a factor of ten greater than the deals Buffett and Munger had done in the 1970s, was becoming routine.

As threatened companies beat a path to Buffett's door, he began to get a reputation as an insider running a "gentlemanly protection game." His terms for taking on a blocking position were typically tough to the point of harshness: He usually took convertible securities with a high yield and generous conversion terms, with a total return often much higher than was available to any other investor. Graham would not have approved, but Buffett might have retorted that he wasn't relaxing his disciplines—he was providing full value for his investment and would never take on a weak company just because he could get an attractive price.

Not quite. Two juicy raider-blocking deals came to him in 1989, one from Gillette and one from U.S. Air, and he did them both. The Gillette deal turned out to be very profitable, while U.S. Air was a disaster. But one of Buffett's great charms is that he never makes excuses. As he told his shareholders:

> The worst sort of business is one that grows rapidly, requires significant capital to engender the growth, and then earns little or no money. Think airlines. . . . Indeed, if a far-sighted capitalist had been present at Kitty Hawk, he would have done his successors a huge favor by shooting Orville [Wright] down.
>
> The airline industry's demand for capital ever since that first flight has been insatiable. Investors have poured money into a bottomless pit. . . . And I, to my shame, participated in this foolishness when I had Berkshire buy U.S. Air preferred stock in 1989. As the ink was drying on our check, the company went into a tailspin and before long our preferred dividend was no longer being paid. But then we got very lucky. In one of the recurrent, but always misguided, bursts of optimism for airlines, we were actually able to sell our shares in 1998 for a hefty gain. In the decade following our sale, the company went bankrupt. Twice.

The most fateful deal, for Buffett personally, was Salomon. Recall that in 1976, "Solly" boss John Gutfreund had done Buffett a huge favor by underwriting a capital raise for a struggling GEICO. A decade later, Salomon had vaulted to the top ranks of investment banks, and Gutfreund had been crowned "King of Wall Street." Business lines, and expenses, proliferated. Inevitably, as Wall

Street's surge abated, Salomon found itself overextended, under-managed, and with poor controls. Then in 1986, Minorco, a South African company based in Bermuda with a controlling block of stock in Salomon,* announced that it was planning to sell its shares to Ronald Perelman, a well-known corporate raider.

Facing a revolt by his own chiefs, Gutfreund called Buffett, who came through immediately, taking a $700 million block of preferred, although he exacted a typically exorbitant price—counting the dividend, and the likely value of the stock conversion feature, the issue was designed to deliver a 15 percent overall return. Salomon bankers were shocked at the terms, but faced with a choice of Buffett or Perelman, they took Buffett.

The Salomon acquisition was very much a crony deal. Buffett did not like Wall Street, although he was a trader and liked Solly's trading operations. But he detested the complex deals, the complex instruments, and especially the new classes of derivatives. He thought they increased risk and transferred far too much unearned income from companies and working people to the sharp-suited guys in the glass-covered towers. His distaste for the Street notwithstanding, he was still happy to bet on his friend Gutfreund.

His pleasure in the transaction disappeared fast. Gutfreund moved very aggressively to shore up the firm, discontinuing marginal businesses, laying off hundreds of people, pulling back on its risks. Then, like other firms, Salomon took a big hit in the 1987 stock

---

* Minorco's interest came through a 1981 acquisition of Salomon by Phibro, a global commodities trader. Minorco was an owner of Phibro. Phibro was supposed to be the dominant partner in the new Phibro/Salomon, but with Gutfreund as co-CEO. Acquiring Gutfreund as a partner was like reeling a shark into a rowboat. Within a couple of years, the Phibro managers were all gone, Gutfreund was sole CEO, and the name was changed back to Salomon Inc.

market crash. The stock price fell sharply, although Buffett's fat preferred dividend was not in danger. At a subsequent compensation committee meeting that Buffett attended, the committee voted to reprice employee stock options so they wouldn't be hurt by the downturn. Buffett was utterly outraged—shareholders were being hurt! Why were employees a privileged class? From that point, although he stayed on the board, he shifted into a passive role. He still liked Gutfreund and wasn't worried about his investment, but he had little interest in the business.

Disappointment in the reality of Salomon was assuaged by a stupendous performance in the rest of the Berkshire portfolio. Toward the end of the decade, Buffett and Munger began buying very large positions in Coca-Cola stock. This was another company that didn't meet the normal Graham investing criteria, but as they watched Coke extend its franchise to the remotest parts of the world, they could see a fountain of future earnings—and were splendidly right. Berkshire closed out 1989 with a $1.5 billion pickup in book value, or 44 percent on a per-share basis. It capped a golden decade for the company: $1,000 invested in Berkshire on January 1, 1980, was worth $12,774 at the end of 1989.

SOMETIMES EVEN BILLIONAIRES WALK ON THORNS

The investment in Salomon, however, came back to haunt Buffett, causing one of the most difficult periods of his business career. In very compressed form, here is the sequence of events:

Salomon was a "primary dealer," one of a small number of elite firms privileged to bid directly at government bond auctions. All other dealers bought their bonds from the primaries. To avoid one primary cornering the market, the government imposed a 35 percent limit on the share of an issue that a single firm could take for resale. Later, in part because of gaming by Salomon, the rule was tightened so no primary could even *bid* for more than a 35 percent share. The bidding limit did not apply, however, to bids on behalf of customers.

In February 1991, the head of Salomon's government bond desk, a young trader named Paul Mozer, took an excess share of an auction by bidding in the name of fake customer accounts. In April, he got a notice that the government was investigating those trades and told his boss, John Meriwether, later of Long-Term Capital Management (LTCM) fame. Meriwether told a handful of other executives, and they informed Gutfreund. They all agreed they should report it immediately, but no one did. (The failure fell especially on Gutfreund's shoulders, because protocol would require a call from him to the New York Fed chief, E. Gerald Corrigan.) Mozer said it was his only offense, promised never to do it again, and was allowed to remain as head of the government desk. As the weeks went by, the threat of an investigation seemed to recede.

A month later, in May, Mozer used similar tactics to execute a "corner" on the 2-year Treasury note issue—taking 85 percent of the issue according to later press reports. Losses by other dealers may have been as much as $100 million. In fact, Mozer's bosses had suspected he was up to something in May, and tried to limit his funds, but he outwitted them too. But they didn't fire him, and banked a very large profit from his trade.

But as rumors of the corner flew wildly around Wall Street, Salomon held an internal inquiry and found evidence of a corner, including a pre-auction dinner between Mozer and two hedge fund managers who bid alongside him in the squeeze. But they accepted Mozer's denial that he had done anything intentionally. In June, Gutfreund met with a Treasury official, expressed apologies for the apparent squeeze and offered to cooperate in any kind of remedial action, but insisted that Salomon had not intentionally violated any rules. He also did not mention the Mozer incident from February. In July, upon notification that the Justice Department was investigating the May squeeze, Gutfreund asked his outside law firm, Wachtell Lipton, to take another look at Mozer's trading. They reported that Mozer had resorted to false bids to exceed his bidding limits at least five times. Then in the summer, Salomon learned that the SEC was investigating the squeeze.

Salomon decided to put out a press release conceding that Mozer had been breaking the rules. When it was read to Buffett before issuance, he got the impression that it was a minor event. On August 9, Salomon executives had a conference call with Corrigan and SEC officials, in which they laid out what they knew of Mozer's trading. Corrigan was shocked that they had withheld the earlier information from him. Some disciplinary action was clearly inevitable, but he expected that they'd be quickly back to him with the details of their housecleaning.

Three days went by, and Corrigan heard nothing, but on August 12, the story of the May corner broke in the *Wall Street Journal*. Still in the dark about Salomon's remedial actions, an exasperated Corrigan sent the firm a letter threatening to withdraw its bidding privileges. That was potentially lethal. Much like Lehman Brothers and Bear Stearns in 2008, Salomon was leveraged at nearly 40:1 ($4 billion in equity supporting $150 billion in assets), and funded itself almost entirely in the short-term money markets. The loss of its role as the lead government primary dealer would raise questions about its creditworthiness. Even a temporary disruption in overnight funding could bankrupt it within a few days.

Salomon executives had a very unpleasant conversation with Corrigan on the thirteenth and started drafting a completely disclosing press release. Board members were ostensibly brought completely up to date. But they were still not told of Gutfreund's less-than-candid June meeting at the Treasury, or about the effective death threat from Corrigan. By the sixteenth, with headlines blaring that Salomon was on the brink of failure, customers were withdrawing trading accounts, and traders were having trouble rolling over short-term borrowings. Gutfreund, finally recognizing that the firm's life was at stake, decided he had to resign and asked Buffett to take over as chairman. Nothing could have been less palatable to Buffett, but he understood that he probably was the only person with a reputation that might by itself restore confidence. So he agreed. To his infinite later embarrassment, he still wasn't told about the Corrigan letter.

Buffett flew to New York for a tough interview with Corrigan. Gutfreund and a second executive agreed to resign. Meriwether resigned the next day. Mozer had been fired. But the firm was in turmoil. Buffett started interviewing internal candidates for CEO and selected Deryck Maughan, a respected Englishman who was untainted by the scandal.

As Buffett was about to take over the chairmanship, he received a note from the Treasury that Salomon would indeed be suspended as a primary dealer. Buffett spent a day calling all his contacts—Treasury Secretary Nicholas Brady and Alan Greenspan among others—but Corrigan would not be moved, and he didn't believe that Salomon would really go under. Buffett finally played his hole card—he would refuse the chairmanship, which was *sure* to sink

Salomon. Corrigan relented, and the Treasury agreed that Salomon could bid for its own accounts, but not for customers, enough of a cosmetic to defuse the worst fears.

Buffett saved Salomon, although he was miserable the entire time. The staff hated him for slashing perquisites and bonuses, never offering a hint of gratitude that he had saved their jobs. He failed to comprehend the Wall Street ethos that it was all about the employees, not the shareholders. At one priceless meeting, a public relations firm came in to make a presentation on handling the crisis. Buffett showed them the door in disgust. "It isn't that we're misunderstood, for Christ's sake," he said. "We don't have a 'public relations' problem. We have a problem with what we *did.*"[12]

Buffett's strategy, which was probably founded on his mistrust of the Salomon culture, was simple. Charlie Munger's law firm came in to do a complete minesweeping review of trading. Buffett pledged to the SEC and to Justice that he would share with them everything that he found, incriminating or not. At first they thought that was incredible but eventually realized that he meant it. And he lived up to it. He took the same approach at congressional hearings—he would disclose to anyone in authority anything he knew as soon as he knew it. (It was at one of the Senate hearings that he learned for the first time, to his shock and anger, about Corrigan's August 12 letter.)

It took months, but in May 1992, the authorities decided not to prosecute Salomon. The firm paid $290 million in fines and penalties, huge by previous standards, but quite modest given the circumstances. Gutfreund and some other executives paid small fines and were temporarily suspended from the industry. Mozer served a four-month term in prison and was banned from the industry for life. Salomon's full dealing privileges were restored.

Buffett, finally, had won his release from purgatory. While he stayed on the board, he stepped down as interim chairman. Maughan was appointed chairman and CEO of the investment bank, Salomon Brothers Inc., and to the Street's surprise, Bob Denham, the lawyer from Munger's firm who had led Buffett's investigation of Salomon's problems, succeeded Buffett as chairman of the holding company, but in a non-executive role. Buffett felt only relief at dropping his executive role at Salomon, but to the world at large he had become a legend.

Four years later, Salomon turned a huge profit for Berkshire when Sandy Weill bought it for Travelers, soon to become Citigroup.

BOOMS AND BUSTS

Markets were kind in the 1990s. Economists and politicians argued over which policies, which presidents, or if just Alan Greenspan deserved the credit. The truth is that none of them mattered that much. Everything was going right for America. The baby boom generation that had caused such disruption in the 1960s and 1970s had entered their high-productivity, high-saving forties and fifties. The over-sixty-five population was flat, since it was absorbing the low-birth cohort of the 1930s. The seas of government red ink, once stretching "as far as the eye can see," were rapidly moving toward surplus—mostly because high social security taxes were generating big trust fund surpluses. On top of that, forty years of government investment produced the Internet, a truly revolutionary technology that for a time existed only in America.

The S&P 500 ended 1990 not much above 300; eight years later, it passed 1,000—an annual gain of about 15 percent, and a fairly smooth one at that. Buffett, as usual, did much better, compounding at more than 30 percent, for an eightfold gain over the same period. Berkshire's 1998 net worth pickup of $25.9 billion brought its total value to more than $57 billion.* Buffett's own wealth, according to *Forbes*, ballooned to $36 billion, solidly in second place behind his good friend Bill Gates, who clocked in at an unassailable $90 billion.

There were nearly 48,000 people employed in Berkshire Hathaway companies, up 9,500 over the previous year, mostly due to acquisitions. Such growth, Buffett lamented, was causing "corporate bloat" in Omaha. "World headquarters," as Buffett liked to call it, had 12.8 people, up from 12 in 1997. The ".8," he went on, "doesn't refer to me or Charlie: We have a new person in accounting working four days a week. Despite this alarming trend . . . our after-tax overhead last year was about $3.5 million, or well under one basis point (.01 of 1 percent) of the assets we manage."[13] Operating earnings were about $1.9 billion, two-thirds from insurance, and the rest from a grab bag of retail companies, flight

---

* In fact, this was a gross understatement. Buffett always values Berkshire at its after-tax "book value," essentially the net value of its assets. At the end of 2007, Berkshire stock was trading at about twice its book value, so shareholder gains were much higher than Buffett's reports suggest. (As of mid-March 2009, in the depths of the market crash, Berkshire's stock is hovering just above end-2008 book.) Buffett's valuation methods produce some reporting quirks. When Buffett purchases a company with stock, the stock is valued at its market price, not the (usually) lower book value. As a consequence, Buffett is getting more book value than he is giving up, inflating the average book value of the remaining shares. Buffett also breaks with traditional Street practice through his preference for paying with cash, even when the market price of Berkshire stock is high. Most firms think of stock as the cheapest acquisition currency. Buffett takes exactly the opposite view. Cash earns him nothing except money market returns, while shares should compound at Buffett rates. (And what does it say about executive confidence if they regard their stock as cheaper currency than cash? Have they cheated their shareholders?)

services, the Buffalo newspaper, and others. Capital gains from investments were $2.5 billion. The big winners were Coca-Cola, Walt Disney (which had bought Capital Cities/ABC), Gillette, and Wells Fargo.

John Meriwether came back into Buffett's life in 1994 with LTCM. Exiled from Salomon, he was pulling together the smartest traders in the world, and backing them with certified geniuses. His partners Robert Merton and Myron Scholes had shared an economics Nobel for inventing some of the foundational mathematics of modern investing. Meriwether raised a stunning $1.25 billion for the fund, despite hefty investment charges of 2 percent of assets plus a quarter of the trading profits. Unlike many hedge fund managers, however, the partners also committed most of their personal net worth, and some even borrowed heavily to increase their initial stake. Meriwether wanted Buffett as a lead investor, and made a presentation to him and Munger in Omaha. LTCM's strategy was to bet on small misalignments in pricing of similar standard instruments, which almost always came back to normal in the near term. The winnings from such bets were small, but they were short-term and you could amplify them with leverage. The math showed that you would take a substantial loss only once a century or so. Buffett and Munger were impressed with the LTCM partner smarts, but declined. They didn't invest in other people's funds.

LTCM is now a classic case of "fat tails" in finance. Portfolio math mimics diffusion physics—a scattergram of the outcomes from trillions of small random movements maps smoothly onto a bell curve. In well-behaved markets, finance looks much the same. But markets are rarely well-behaved for long, and big deviations from the norm happen very frequently in finance—the finance bell curve, that is, has fat tails. When Russia defaulted on its sovereign bonds in 1998, it was a fat tail for LTCM, and it was on the wrong side of the trade, with very heavy leverage.

LTCM partners made a futile attempt to lure Buffett back. The Fed belatedly realized that LTCM had leveraged up to a gross position of more than $100 million, almost all of it borrowed, and was taking brutal losses. Alan Greenspan, the Fed chairman, later told Congress that its failure would have had the potential to "impair the economies of many nations, including our own."[14] Jerry Corrigan almost worked out an arrangement whereby Goldman would take over the positions, backed by an estimated $3.5 billion in financing from Buffett. Buffett was willing, and actually made a written offer even though he was on vacation in remote Alaska. The deal never came off, probably because Meriwether didn't want Buffett as his employer again. Corrigan finally raised the funds by strong-arming a consortium of twenty banks, which made no more than a small profit on the workout. Buffett summed up the episode as an "example of what happens when you get (1) a dozen people with an average IQ of 160; (2) working in a field in which they collectively have 250 years of experience; (3) operating with a huge percentage of their net worth in the business; (4) employing a ton of leverage."[15]

Buffett had a few uncomfortable years at the height of the dot-com boom. His rule was never invest in something you don't understand. He was a friend and admirer of Robert Noyce, a co-founder of Intel, but he still didn't understand Intel, so he passed on it. Berkshire grossly underperformed the S&P 500 in 1999, gaining just a half percent, against the S&P's 21 percent, only the fourth time that had happened in thirty-five years. At the 1999 Sun Valley conference, an annual event bringing together most of the heaviest hitters in media and finance, Buffett gave a typically charming but bleak talk on the market's overvaluation, which most of the conferees seemed to read as hopelessly out of date. He stuck to his guns, although it hurt him to get complaints from Berkshire shareholders for missing the tech boom. There was a repeat performance, however, at the 2001 conference in the midst of the dot-com implosion. He didn't rub it in—that was never his way—but he enjoyed the new attentiveness of the audience.

Two-thousand-one was a terrible year, on multiple counts, and was the first time that Berkshire showed a loss, although it still outperformed the S&P. But Buffett always did well in downturns, and his 2002 performance was a superb 10 percent against the S&P's 22 percent loss. As the market continued to stagger, Buffett and Munger were snapping up companies right and left. At Berkshire's 2007 annual meeting, they told their shareholders that they owned 76 companies with 233,000 employees. The big earners, both in revenues and in producing the precious "float," came from the insurance operations, but there was also a powerful utility sector. Buffett's pride and joy, however, was a "motley" collection of businesses making "everything from lollipops to motor homes" that returned an average 23 percent on book equity while using very little leverage. Some of his old favorites were still star performers. He and Charlie had bought See's Candies in 1972 for $25 million. In 2007, its sales were $383 million and it turned an $82 million profit. Mrs. B's furniture mart had sales of $400 million; it was one of the two biggest furniture stores in the country and, as always, one of the most profitable. The book value of Berkshire had grown to $120 billion, even though its stock portfolio, still worth double what he had paid for it, had fallen considerably in the market downdraft.[16]

A special word on Berkshire's casualty insurance operations, as exemplifying the unique, but still common-sense genius of Warren Buffett. They are a core contributor to the company's earnings and to its "float," or excess cash held against payout liabilities, but available for current investment. As Buffett frequently points out, casualty insurance is a commodity business that competes on price. The attraction of the upfront cash inflows, however, almost always triggers such fierce price competition that the industry as a whole is usually unprofitable. Episodes of extreme underpricing are also invariably followed by episodes of extreme scarcity as bloodied companies withdraw to repair their balance sheets. The Berkshire rule is that you never play the volume game. You price-to-profit, regardless of the competition—so you concede volume during the price-war cycle, but then take huge share when the rest of the industry is licking its wounds. In one six-year period, for example, Berkshire's National Indemnity Company's annual underwriting volumes varied by more than tenfold. But they designed the company for volume volatility—overhead is very lean, so staff are assured that they won't be laid off during the downturns, and losses on underwriting are rare. Roughly four years out of five, the insurance "float" comes to them free.

LORD WARREN THE WISE

As Buffett's image transmuted from country slicker to all-seeing guru, his annual shareholder letters took on the aura of pronouncements from the mountain top. And deservedly so, for they put the daily follies of Wall Street, accounting, and management practices under the cold laser of a very uncommon common sense. Herewith a selection:

The Wall Street Language Game

"Some years back, our competitors were known as 'leveraged buy-out operators.' But LBO became a bad name. So in true Orwellian fashion, the buyout firms decided to change their moniker. . . . Their new label became 'private equity,' a name that turns the facts upside-down: A purchase of a business by these firms almost invariably results in dramatic *reductions* in the equity portion of the acquiree's capital structure compared to that previously existing. A number of these acquirees, purchased only two to three years ago, are now in mortal danger because of the debt piled on them by their private-equity buyers. . . . The private-equity firms, it should be noted, are not rushing in to inject the equity their wards now desperately need. Instead they're keeping their remaining funds *very* private."—2008

"[T]he *least* independent directors are likely to be those who receive an important fraction of their annual income from the fees they receive for board service. . . . Yet these are the very board members most often classed as 'independent.'"—2004

"Bad terminology is the enemy of good thinking. When companies or investment professionals use terms like 'EBITDA' and 'pro forma,' they want you to accept concepts that are dangerously flawed. (In golf, my score is frequently below par on a *pro forma* basis: I have firm plans to 'restructure' my putting stroke and therefore only count the swings I take before reaching the green.)"—2001

"Managers thinking about accounting issues should never forget one of Abraham Lincoln's favorite riddles: 'How many legs does a dog have if you call his tail a leg? The answer: 'Four, because calling a tail a leg does not make it a leg.'"—1992

Accounting Outrages

"I can assure you that the marking errors in the derivatives business have not been symmetrical. Almost invariably, they have favored the trader who was eyeing a multi-million dollar bonus or the CEO who wanted to report impressive 'earnings' (or both). Only much later did shareholders learn that the reported earnings were a sham."—2002

On not expensing grants of stock options: "Think for a moment of the $190 million we are going to spend for advertising at GEICO this year. Suppose that instead of paying cash for our ads, we paid the media in ten-year, at-the-market Berkshire options. Would anyone then care to argue that Berkshire had not borne a cost for advertising, or should not be charged this cost on its books?"—1998

"The distortion *du jour* is the 'restructuring charge,' an accounting entry that can, of course, be legitimate but that too often is a device for manipulating earnings. . . . [A] large chunk of costs that should properly be attributed to a number of years is dumped into a single quarter, typically one already fated to disappoint investors . . . [following] the cynical proposition that Wall Street will not mind if earnings fall short by $5 per share in a given quarter, just as long as this deficiency ensures that quarterly earnings in the future will consistently exceed expectations by five cents per share.

"The dump-everything-in-one-quarter behavior suggests a correspondingly 'bold, imaginative' approach to—golf scores. In his first round of the season, a golfer should ignore his actual performance and simply fill his card with atrocious numbers—double, triple, quadruple bogeys—and then turn in a score of, say, 140. Having established this 'reserve,' [he can subsequently] count his good holes, but not the bad ones [which] should be charged instead to the reserve . . . and will classify our hero as an 80 shooter."—1998

Snake Oil Salesmen

On pension consultants pushing diversification: "[Assume an investor purchased] an interest in, say, 20 percent of the future earnings of a number of outstanding college basketball stars. A handful of these would go on to achieve NBA stardom, and the investor's take from them would soon dominate his royalty stream. To suggest that this investor should sell off portions of his most successful investments simply because they have come to dominate his portfolio is akin to suggesting that the Bulls trade Michael Jordan because he has become so important to the team."—1996

"The disciples of debt told us that [the junk bond collapse] wouldn't happen: Huge debt, we were told, would cause operating managers to focus their efforts as never before, much as a dagger mounted on the steering wheel of a car could be expected to make its driver to proceed with intensified care. We'll acknowledge that such an attention-getter would produce a very alert driver. But another certain consequence would be a deadly—and unnecessary—accident if the car hit even the tiniest pothole or sliver of ice. The roads of business are riddled with potholes; a plan that requires dodging them all is a plan for disaster."—1990

"Thus, said the friendly salesman, a diversified portfolio of junk bonds would produce greater net returns than would a portfolio of high-grade bonds. (Beware of past-performance 'proofs' in finance: If history books were the key to riches, the *Forbes* 400 would consist of librarians.). . . . As usual, the Street's enthusiasm for an idea was proportional not to its merit, but rather to the revenue it would produce. Mountains of junk bonds were sold by those who didn't care to those who didn't think—and there was no shortage of either."—1990

"Wall Street welcomed [zero-coupon bonds] with the enthusiasm less-enlightened folks might reserve for the wheel or the plow. Here, finally, was an instrument that would let the Street make deals at prices no longer limited by actual earning power. . . . The zero-coupon . . . bond possesses one additional attraction for the promoter and investment banker, which is that the time elapsing between folly and failure can be stretched out. This is no small benefit. If the period before all costs must be faced is long, promoters can create a string of foolish deals—and take in a lot of fees—before any chickens come home to roost from their earlier ventures."—1989

"[Deal promoters] have throughout time exercised the same judgment and restraint in accepting money that alcoholics have exercised in accepting liquor. At a minimum, therefore, the banker's conduct should rise to that of a responsible bartender who, when necessary, refuses the profit from the next drink to avoid sending a drunk out on the highway. In recent years, unfortunately, many leading investment firms have found bartender morality to be an intolerably restrictive standard."—1989

On "portfolio insurance," or stop-loss selling in the futures markets as stock prices decline: "[The strategy] tells a pension fund or university . . . when it owns a portion of enterprises such as Ford or General Electric [that] . . . the less these companies are valued at, the more vigorously they should be sold. As a 'logical' corollary, the approach commands the institutions to repurchase these companies—*I'm not making this up*—once their prices have rebounded significantly. Considering that huge sums are controlled by managers following such Alice-in-Wonderland practices, is it any surprise that markets sometimes behave in aberrational fashion?" —1987

"Why then, are 'cash-flow' numbers [excluding capital expenditures] so popular today? In answer, we confess our cynicism: we believe these numbers are frequently used by marketers of businesses and securities in attempts to justify the unjustifiable (and therefore sell what should be the unsalable.)"—1986

CEO Follies

"But now [stock] repurchases are all the rage, but are too often made for an unstated and, in our view, ignoble reason: to pump or support the stock price. The shareholder who chooses to sell today, of course, is benefitted. . . . But the *continuing* shareholder is penalized by repurchases above intrinsic value. . . . Sometimes, too, companies say they are repurchasing shares to offset the shares issued when stock options granted at much lower prices are exercised. This 'buy high, sell low' strategy is one many unfortunate investors have employed—but never intentionally! Managements, however, seem to follow this perverse activity very cheerfully."—1999

"The sad fact is that most major acquisitions display an egregious imbalance: They are a bonanza for the shareholders of the acquiree; they increase the income and status of the acquirer's management; and they are a honey pot for the investment bankers and other professionals on both sides. But, alas, they usually reduce the wealth of the acquirer's shareholders, often to a substantial extent."—1994

"[The business] institutional imperative. . . . (1) As if governed by Newton's First Law of Motion, an institution will resist any change in its current direction; (2) Just as work expands to fill available time, corporate projects or acquisitions will materialize to soak up available funds; (3) Any business craving of the leader, however foolish, will be quickly supported by detailed rate-of-return and strategic studies prepared by his troops; and (4) The behavior of peer companies, whether they are expanding, acquiring, setting executive compensation, or whatever, will be mindlessly imitated."—1989

"CEOs rarely tell their shareholders that they have assembled a bunch of turkeys to run things. Their reluctance to do so makes for some strange annual reports. Oftentimes, in his shareholders' letter, a CEO will go on for pages detailing corporate performance that is woefully inadequate. He will nonetheless end with a warm paragraph describing his managerial colleagues as 'our most precious asset.' Such comments sometimes make you wonder what the other assets can possibly be."—1987

"[Why acquisitions?] (1) Leaders, business or otherwise, seldom are deficient in animal spirits and often relish increased activity and challenge. . . . (2) Most organizations, business or otherwise, measure themselves, are measured by others, and compensate their managers far more by the yardstick of size than by any other yardstick. . . . (3) Many managements apparently were overexposed in impressionable childhood years to the story in which the imprisoned handsome prince is released from a toad's body by a kiss from a beautiful princess."—1981

Corporate Governance

[Each investment company fund, which are mostly mutual funds, must have a board of non-employee directors who are fiduciaries for the investors] "Many thousands of investment-company boards meet annually to carry out the vital job of selecting who will look after the interests of the millions of owners they represent. Year after year the directors of Fund A select manager A, Fund B directors select manager B, etc., in a zombie-like process that makes a mockery of stewardship."—2002

"It's almost impossible, for example, in a boardroom populated by well-mannered people to raise the question of whether the CEO should be replaced. It's equally awkward to question a proposed acquisition that has been endorsed by the CEO. Finally, when the compensation committee—armed, as always, with a report from a highly-paid consultant—reports on a mega grant of options to the CEO, it would be like belching at the dinner table for a director to suggest that the committee reconsider."—2002

Miscellaneous Gems

On CEO complaints that bureaucrats spend taxpayer money as if it were their own: "Salomon . . . had a barber, Jimmy by name, who came in weekly to give free haircuts to the top brass. . . . Then, because of a cost-cutting drive, patrons were told to pay their own way. One top executive . . . went immediately to a one-every-three-weeks schedule."—2006

"The Gotrocks Fable": Gotrocks is a family that owns all corporate America. Each year after taxes, their net worth goes up by $700 billion. The family shares the money equably and all grow fabulously wealthy. Then some members decide they should be able to do better than the others, so they hire "Helpers," who for a fee will improve their position by trading. Since the family already owns everything, they are just rearranging assets. But the additional costs reduce the family's net wealth, and most end up worse off. So they hire more sophisticated, and highly paid, consultants, eventually graduating to paying hedge fund and private equity management fees. An arms race starts as family members start hiring more and more sophisticated Helpers. Soon, much like today, the fees to the Helpers consume 20 percent of the earnings of business. Buffett concludes the sad tale by proposing Newton's Fourth Law of Motion: "For investors as a whole, returns decrease as motion increases."—2005

On investor and CEO herding: "[L]emmings as a class may be derided, but never does an *individual* lemming get criticized." —2004

"[Derivatives] can exacerbate trouble that a corporation has run into for completely unrelated reasons. This pile-on effect occurs because many derivative contracts require that a company suffering a credit downgrade immediately supply collateral to counterparties . . . [which can] impose an unexpected and enormous demand for cash collateral. . . . It all becomes a spiral that can lead to a corporate meltdown."—2002

[Buffett's warning is a precise description of what happened to AIG six years later.]

On the long tail of casualty insurance losses: A family member asked his sister why he was still getting bills for their father's funeral several years after the event. "'Oh,' she replied, 'I forgot to tell you. We buried dad in a rented suit.'"—2001

On Berkshire's investment strategy: "We try to *price* rather than *time* purchases. In our view, it is folly to forego buying shares in an outstanding business whose long-term future is predictable, because short-term worries about an economy or a stock market that we know to be unpredictable. Why scrap an informed decision because of an uninformed guess?"—1994

On budgeting: "Charlie and I do not believe in flexible operating budgets. . . . We neither understand the adding of unneeded people or activities because profits are booming, nor the cutting of essential people or activities because profitability is shrinking. . . . Our goal is to do what makes sense for Berkshire's customers and employees at all times, and never to add the unneeded. ('But what about the CORPORATE JET?' you rudely ask. Well, occasionally, a man must rise above principle.)"—1987

[Buffett and Munger named the jet *The Indefensible*.]

On casualty insurers: "In most businesses, of course, insolvent companies run out of cash. Insurance is different; you can be broke but flush. Since cash comes in at the inception of an insurance policy and the losses are paid much later, insolvent insurers don't run out of cash until long after they have run out of net worth. In fact, these 'walking dead' often redouble their efforts to write business, accepting almost any price or risk, simply to keep the cash flowing in."—1984

On inflation: "One friendly but sharp-eyed commentator on Berkshire has pointed out that our book value at the end of 1964 would have bought about one-half ounce of gold and, fifteen years later, after we have plowed back all earnings along with much blood, sweat, and tears, the book value produced will buy about the same half ounce."—1979

COMES THE CRASH

Berkshire Hathaway had a difficult year in 2008, prompting the same worries as a decade before that "Buffett was losing his touch." For the full year, Berkshire's per share book value dropped by 9.6 percent, only its second book-value reduction ever, and the biggest. (Measured by the S&P 500 Index, which is Buffett's performance target, however, it did extremely well, beating the index by 27.4 percent—but Buffett took no pride in that.)

The book value reduction was driven entirely by two items. The first, and the biggest, was the fall in unrealized appreciation of the Berkshire investment portfolio—all the favorite Buffett stocks like Coca-Cola and American Express were hit hard in the market. While he kicked himself for some purchases and sales (or non-sales), Buffett doesn't generally worry about stock market prices;

his focus is on long-term net worth. The market value of those shares continued to fall sharply through the first quarter.

The second source of book value loss was a net $14.4 billion loss in derivatives. What in the world is Warren Buffett, the scourge of derivatives as "financial weapons of mass destruction," doing with positions that affect earnings that much? Read the fine print in the financial footnotes, and you see that he knows exactly what he is doing.

The biggest hit was $10 billion in "mark-to-market" losses on "equity index puts." Berkshire has entered into options contracts with institutional stock holders to limit their losses against specific stock indexes. Contracts are written with reference to the S&P 500 in the United States, and to the comparable indexes in London, Europe, and Japan. These are "European" options. Each counter-party who makes an upfront payment is guaranteed that on a *specific* future day, its reference index will not be below its level on the day of the contract. The future date on all contracts is between nineteen and twenty-eight years from contract execution, with an average remaining life of thirteen-and-a-half years. As of the end of 2008, Berkshire had been paid $4.7 billion upfront to guarantee some $37 billion in portfolios. Since the upfront payment is 13 percent of the total portfolio, Berkshire would not take any losses unless the average reference indexes were 13 percent lower on the future reference dates compared to the execution dates—without giving effect to the free use of the $4.7 billion for all of those years. (Rises or falls in an index prior to the reference date are irrelevant. The index level on that specific reference day is all that matters.)

Why the "loss?" Berkshire is using the most conservative possible accounting, booking as a non-cash loss the net payment (loss payout less fee) they *would have had* to make if the reference date were on December 31, 2008. Certainly, it is *possible*—if the United States and the rest of the world slip into a Japan-style, decade-plus-long slump—that Berkshire would end up making big pay-outs, but thirteen years is a long time, and it is far from a likely case. For the maximum possible payout of $37 billion to be required, all the reference indexes would have to be at *zero* on the reference dates.*

The price of Berkshire stock dropped sharply in 2008, but Buffett has never cared about his stock price. He tracks his company's book value or net assets, a hard number that anyone can read off the financials. He's not in the business of playing markets. In short, there is no evidence that, at age seventy-eight, Buffett is at all off his game. As this book goes to press, however, one rating agency (Fitch) reduced Berkshire Hathaway's rating from AAA to AA+, citing both the derivative losses and the company's dependency on Buffett.

PRESIDENTIAL ADVISER

At a critical juncture in the 2008 presidential campaign, when Barack Obama was struggling to establish his bona fides in eco-

---

* Buffett is taking a very conservative valuation view, far more so than accounting standards require. The puts are all tailored instruments classified as "Level 3" assets that have no relevant market measurement standard. So Buffett would be free to value them solely by an internal model that, say, estimated the range of settlement prices on the contract dates. Why would the option buyers pay so much for the contracts? Presumably they are institutions, like many corporate pension funds, that care very much about taking mark-to-market losses, and are willing to pay to place a floor under the value of their equity holdings.

nomic policy, both Buffett and Paul Volcker became highly visible faces at Obama economic events, like an October presentation of an early stimulus plan.

How did he think Obama would do? Buffett was asked in a wide-ranging PBS interview. "I don't think there's anybody better that you could have in the presidency than Barack Obama at this time. He understands economics. He's a very smart guy. He's a cool rational-type of thinker."

What kind of advice was he giving him on the economy? "(Laughing.) I was telling him business was going to be *awful*." But he went on, "[H]e's got the right ideas. He believes in the same things I believe in: America's best days are ahead and that we've got a great economic machine; it's sputtering now. And he believes there could be a more equitable job done in distributing the rewards of this great machine. But he doesn't need my advice on anything."

What economic policies would work best? "The answer is nobody knows. The economists don't know. . . . You're going to use every weapon you have in fighting it. And people, they do not know exactly what the effects are. Economists like to talk about it, but in the end they've been very, very wrong, and most of them, in recent years on this. . . . We do know over time the American machine works wonderfully and it will work wonderfully again."

Are we creating new problems? "Always. . . . I mean you are giving a medicine dosage to the patient on a scale that we haven't seen in this country. And there will be aftereffects and they can't be predicted exactly. But certainly the potential is there for inflationary consequences that would be significant."

What are the trade-offs? "Well . . . the trade-off basically is that you risk setting in motion forces that will be very hard to stop in terms of inflation down the road and you are creating an imbalance between revenues and expenses in the government that is a lot easier to create than it will be to correct later on, but those are problems worth taking on—but you don't get a free lunch."

Do we need better regulation? "Once the real estate market became a bubble, I don't think anyone could have stopped it. When everybody in the country is convinced that their house price is going to rise indefinitely, and every bank starts giving really easy payment plans, then you're going to have a bubble."

Could better rules prevent that? "Well, there are probably some new rules needed but the regulatory system I don't think could have stopped this. . . . Once the American public, the U.S. Congress, all the commentators, the media, everybody else started thinking house prices could do nothing but go up, you were creating a bubble. . . . I mean you had 22 trillion dollars probably worth of homes. It was the biggest asset of most American families and you let them borrow 100 percent in many cases . . . and you let them refi up to where they kept taking out more and more and treating it as an ATM machine. . . . The bubble was going to happen."

But everyone is demanding more rules. "Well . . . you just require that anybody who bought a house to put 20 percent down and make sure that the payments were not more than a third of their income. Now we would not have a big bust ever in real estate again. . . . [But now] you got a home yourself and now you're saying a guy with a 5 percent down payment shouldn't get one. So I think it's very tough to put rules out. . . . It's like I say in economics: you can't do just one thing, and where the balance is struck on that will be a political question. My guess is that it won't be struck particularly well, but that's just the nature of politics."[17]

When I started this book, I was really curious to learn Buffett's thoughts on re-regulation and restarting the economy, the more so since he had been such a visible presence both during the Obama campaign, and during the early transition. I was quite disappointed to be told that he was not giving interviews during my writing window. That was hardly a surprise, for he had just spent five years cooperating in the production of Alice Schroeder's fine *Snowball*, which he might fairly have regarded as a vaccine against future interviewers. At nine-hundred-some pages, *Snowball* does indeed cover almost anything one could reasonably want to know about Buffett or his methods, except this one topic.

At the same time, having read all the available Buffett shareholder letters, plus a great deal more about him, I was pretty sure that an interview on regulation would be anticlimactic, that he would say more or less what he said to the PBS interviewer, because it's not the kind of question that engages him. (Once the interviewer's policy questions were out of the way, he happily switched to talking about Ben Graham.)

Roger Lowenstein, in his own fine biography of Buffett—which Buffett did not cooperate in—pushes at the question of why Buffett keeps paying homage to Graham when he so frequently deviates from Graham's principles. He suggests that Buffett is a Graham disciple less in technique than in temperament and attitude, which may be more important. I think that's right. The real essence of Graham, as filtered by Buffett, isn't the detailed rules. It's just a no-flapdoodle approach to investing. Forget the theories, keep it real, keep it simple. Leaving aside the atmospherics of Buffett's acquisitions, his principles were pretty consistent—look at value, find businesses that should work over the long term, and where the economic model is clean and straightforward.

That is a mindset that doesn't translate well to regulatory questions. Regulation is a shadow game of if-we-do-this-then-they-will, etc. Buffett's world is one where he follows his own course and doesn't give a fig what everyone else does.

Contrast that with George Soros, who is a master of shadow worlds—what else was the pound coup?—and who is very interested in regulation. Throughout the crisis, in a stream of statements and columns, he has produced a number of ingenious, and usually practical, proposals. It's just one more axis of the Soros-Buffett contrast. The two most successful investors in history, approaching their trade from completely different directions, and each of them thinking about government and regulation in exactly the same way he thinks about everything else.

VOLCKER

*P*aul Volcker's eight-year chairmanship of the Federal Reserve Board was the central episode of his professional career, and is universally recognized as one of the great public service performances of recent history. If there were a Nobel Prize for government service, Volcker's would be one of the names on the short list.[1]

Volcker has spent almost his entire professional life dealing with financial crises—bank failures, currency collapses, global imbalances, economic crashes. In persona and presence, he is central casting's notion of the global banker—tall (six foot seven), imposing, gruff, but unfailingly courteous, and with a fine sense of humor in private. The crises that defined his career can almost all be understood as part of the backwash from the breakdown of the "Bretton Woods" system of international finance created at the close of World War II, and the failure to construct a reliable replacement system. Volcker was the field general in charge of America's international monetary policy during most of unwinding of Bretton Woods; and at the Fed, of course, he controlled the monetary machinery itself.

Volcker comes from solid German stock; all four of his grandparents were immigrants. His mother's parents ran a dry goods store in upstate New York; on his father's side, his grandmother was a school teacher in Brooklyn, and his grandfather was a tea and coffee wholesaler. Grandfather Adolph Volcker—six foot four, three hundred pounds, with an imposing handlebar mustache—

passed on his size. Paul's three sisters—he was the youngest child of four—were all six feet tall in their early teens.

Paul was named after his father, who was a civil engineer—from Rensselaer Polytechnic—who became a city manager, and was recruited to Teaneck, New Jersey, a leafy suburb across the Hudson from New York City, in 1930. His mother, Alma, went to Vassar, graduating as valedictorian with a degree in chemistry. After a year working as a teaching assistant, she married Paul, and as was the rule in the 1920s, became a homemaker. She was very literate, very involved in the community, very involved in her husband's work.

By all accounts, Paul's father was a superb city manager, the opposite of a politician. Taking over Teaneck in the early days of the Depression, he cleaned up its finances, lowered taxes, and put in a master plan that he followed carefully. His devotion to the job was all-consuming. There were nighttime meetings on most weekdays, and on Saturdays and Sundays, he drove around Teaneck taking notes on a tattered park, a broken light, misplaced trash. He was organized and careful: An admiring obituary in the local paper summed him up as a man who "seldom if ever made snap judgments."

Paul's parents, both in word and deed, epitomized the ideal of public service, one that he absorbed from an early age. In Teaneck, his father was an important man on a modest salary. He was on a first-name basis with all the important men of the town, but the Volckers did not belong to the country club, and Paul's father would never have taken a gift membership. Decades later, the wealthy and powerful, the great and the good, hung on Paul's every word—he who wore rumpled suits, had hot dogs for lunch, and went home to a tiny bachelor's pad because his wife was too ill to accompany him back to Washington.

When Paul graduated from high school, it was assumed that he would study engineering, like his father, and he had been accepted at Rensselaer. But Paul made a spur-of-the-moment application to Princeton and was accepted there too. (In 1945, the madly competitive scramble for college places was far in the future.) Despite his father's doubts, he went to Princeton, and discovered both that he was a very good student and that he enjoyed economics—the policy part, more than the mathematical modeling. His senior thesis was on the Federal Reserve.

Graduate school depended on scholarships. Paul spent two years at Harvard's Littauer School (now the John F. Kennedy School of Government), where he combined economics and political science, followed by a year at the London School of Economics. He didn't write a PhD thesis but spent a lot of time learning the operations of the Bank of England. At the party his parents gave him when he returned from England, he met Barbara Bahnson, a doctor's daughter and an undergrad at Pembroke (then the Brown University women's affiliate). They were married two years later. Paul became a staff economist at the Federal Reserve, later moving on to Chase Manhattan Bank.

The narrative arc of Volcker's career is an illuminating counterpoint to the careers of George Soros and Warren Buffett, for Volcker powerfully influenced the environment in which they plied their trade. Government is not just a regulator of finance. It creates and manipulates money and sovereign debt, the raw material of finance, and establishes the legal and contractual environment in which financiers operate. The major milestones in Volcker's resume—the breakup of Bretton Woods, the ensuing explosion of money and credit, the inflation of the superbank bubble, and the ballooning of private debt—shaped the business lives of everyone.

UNWINDING BRETTON WOODS: THE KENNEDY YEARS

Volcker joined the staff of Robert Roosa, the Treasury undersecretary for monetary affairs in the new Kennedy administration, in 1962 and was appointed deputy undersecretary the following year. Roosa's office was a new one, created expressly to deal with early unravelings of the postwar financial order. The 1944 Bretton Woods Agreement, hammered out at a conference of all the allied nations, created the operating infrastructure for the postwar global financial system. Inevitably, the system was centered around the United States, since it was the only country that would emerge from the war both unscathed and with its production capacity on wartime steroids. American companies were the only ones geared up to meet postwar global demand; American citizens owned the great bulk of global savings; and the American government controlled most of the world's monetary gold.

The U.S. dollar, fixed at $35 per ounce of gold since 1934, became the de facto international reserve currency, with other currencies fixed relative to the dollar. Exchange rates were supposed to be stable, but non-dollar currencies could and did adjust, albeit infrequently. The International Monetary Fund was created and capitalized by its governing members to act as a liquidity lender for countries in temporary exchange-rate difficulties.

Especially at the outset, it was essential that the United States run chronic current-account deficits—net outflows in its trade and overseas investment accounts—so other countries could acquire the financial reserves to rebuild their banking and credit systems. There were two ways to accomplish that. The first was through outright grants and loans from the United States, as epitomized by the Marshall Plan. The second was for the dollar to be somewhat overvalued relative to other currencies. An overvalued dollar made foreign-sourced goods appear cheap to Americans, and American-made goods expensive for Europeans and Asians. The net effect was a consistent bias toward an American trade deficit, or smaller trade surplus than would have otherwise been the case.

The flaw in Bretton Woods was that it implicitly assumed a continuance of the titanic disproportion between America's and the rest of the world's wealth and productive capacity. When Volcker joined the Treasury, however, the American wealth advantage was rapidly narrowing. Europe was in full recovery mode, growth rates were very high, and alert American businessmen—with George Soros in the lead—wanted to be in on the action. American companies were taking advantage of the dollar's valuation premium to buy up European companies, infuriating France's Charles de Gaulle, who railed against Americans' expropriation of Europe's industrial crown jewels.

In strict economic terms, American international accounts were in very good shape. The trade books were still in healthy surplus, easily financing the large volume of official transfers to support foreign aid and the far-flung Cold War military establishment. The accelerating volume of overseas investing, however, pushed the overall position to a $2 to $3 billion net annual outflow, but that was small relative to American GDP, and consistent with the Bretton Woods objective of recapitalizing the rest of the world.

The problem was the American gold reserve. As the economy and the monetary system expanded steadily, the quantity of circulating dollars grew vastly greater than the physical volume of gold allegedly supporting it. The mismatch between overseas dollar holdings and American gold reserves was like catnip for currency traders, who kept testing America's commitment to the $35 gold peg. The textbook method of beating back currency speculators is to raise interest rates; higher rates would slow U.S. growth and reduce imports at the same time as they attracted dollar balances from abroad. But Kennedy had been elected "to get the country moving again," and higher rates were the last thing he wanted. William McChesney Martin, chairman of the Fed, was a traditionalist and wanted to raise rates; Congress was apoplectic. After floating a number of gambits, the administration finally settled on a tax on foreign securities purchases.

Volcker was in charge of drafting the tax bill, and quickly discovered the yawning gap between thought and action in Washington. Worthy industry after worthy industry showed up, congressional supporters in train, looking for exemptions—until Volcker realized that the accumulating loopholes would vitiate the purpose of the tax. He finally pushed it through as a more or less "pure" bill with only minimal exemptions.

Both he and his masters were delighted to see investment outflows drop sharply almost as soon as the tax went into effect. At least that's what the data showed. But Volcker was also aware that the falloff could be an illusion, for at about the same time as the new tax took effect, there was a sharp uptick in the fledgling "Eurodollar" market. Instead of dollars earned overseas being repatriated to the United States, they were being deposited in foreign banks or in foreign branches of American banks, where they could be reinvested in Europe without the bother of a tax. As the overseas dollars lurked and grew, they were eventually at the root of an entirely new species of crises.

UNWINDING BRETTON WOODS: THE NIXON YEARS

Volcker returned to Chase Manhattan in 1965, then rejoined the Treasury in 1969. He came back to Washington for Roosa's old job as undersecretary for monetary affairs in the new Nixon administration, just in time to preside over the final unraveling of Bretton Woods. In addition to the inherent strains of a one-country global reserve currency, there was a new ideological challenge to the postwar monetary order. That was the rapid ascendance of the "efficient markets hypothesis" of Chicago School monetarists, pushed hard by Milton Friedman. To monetarists, any attempt to manage international currencies was doomed to failure. Bureaucratically fixed rates were certain to be wrong, and would themselves be major impediments to market efficiencies. The best course was simply to allow all currencies to float freely. Market forces would quickly assign an accurate price to every currency; subsequent adjustments would be smooth and continuous, reflecting underlying economic realities. In his retrospective on the period, Volcker sniffs that the Chicago School expectation of smooth adjustment "had not been the experience of the 1930s."[2] At the time, however, one had to concede that the 1930s were possibly a unique episode; *a priori*, it was impossible to show that the monetarists were wrong.

The monetarists' theoretical objections, however, merely reinforced the sense of the sheer impracticality of maintaining the current system. Reserve currency status confers two privileges on the issuing country. The first is that the reserve country's currency has an inflated value in international markets because so many national treasuries must buy it for their reserves. The second is that the reserve country can always borrow abroad in its own currency, so if its international debt ever becomes burdensome, it can pay it off just by printing more currency.*

But the privileges come at a cost. The issuing country implicitly assumes a responsibility to maintain global currency stability, which limits its freedom to undertake expansionary policies at home. Maintaining the gold value of the dollar conflicted with the Kennedy growth imperative in 1962, although it was finessed by the foreign security tax ploy. Starting about 1965, Lyndon Johnson started running big budget deficits to finance the war in Vietnam and his domestic program. The floods of new money were already generating inflationary pressures, as well as drawing currency-

---

* When a non-dollar country borrows in dollars and converts them to its own currency for domestic use, it runs the risk that its currency will fall against the dollar before the loan is paid off, which will increase the pain of the repayment. That was the central mechanism of the 1990s East Asian currency crises. Since the U.S. almost always borrows in dollars, it does not run that risk. In the depths of its 1970s inflation crisis, however, when the dollar was in free-fall, the United States was briefly forced to borrow in marks and yen, since foreign banks did not want to hold dollars.

market assaults on the dollar–gold peg, when Volcker came back to the Treasury.

And once again, the prescribed medicine—raise interest rates and reduce borrowing—was not on the table, for it conflicted with Richard Nixon's desire to win a second presidential term.

The first two years of the Nixon administration were very difficult economic sailing, to the point where the administration was seriously worried about the 1972 election. During the five years of Johnson's presidency, despite the uptick in inflation, the real, or inflation-adjusted, annual rate of growth exceeded 5 percent. But in 1970, growth plunged to near zero, while inflation was scraping 6 percent—dreadful numbers for a campaign launch.[3]

There was little room for maneuver. The 1970 federal deficit was already as big as any Johnson had run, so fiscal stimulation was likely to spill over into more inflation. Rising oil and other imports had pushed U.S. trade accounts into deficit, so dollars were piling up in foreign hands, and global currency traders were mounting ever more aggressive raids.

But few politicians had Nixon's gift for the bold stroke. In August 1971 he helicoptered his entire economics team to Camp David for a weekend that Herbert Stein, a member of the Council of Economic Advisers, predicted "could be the most important meeting in the history of economics"[4] since the New Deal. After the meeting, which was dominated by the outsized Texas Democrat, Treasury Secretary John Connally, Nixon announced that he would cut taxes, impose wage and price controls throughout the economy, impose a tax surcharge on all imports, and rescind the commitment to redeem dollars in gold.

As the Treasury man on monetary matters, Volcker was a major player at Camp David. He remembers it more as a lesson in politics. After the final decisions had been taken, he was charged with drafting Nixon's and Connally's speeches announcing the changes. His draft, he recalled, was "a typical devaluation speech" filled with the "obligatory mea culpas." None of it saw the light of day. The Volcker draft was handed over to über speechwriter William Safire and emerged as a proclamation of "a triumph and a fresh start."[5]

Politically, it was a masterstroke. With price controls in place, Nixon and his Federal Reserve chief, Arthur Burns, could gun up the money supply without worrying about price inflation—both the narrow and broad measures of money jumped by more than 10 percent in 1971, at the time the biggest increase ever. Economic growth obediently revived, and was back up over 5 percent by the 1972 election—just what the political doctors had ordered.

Consumers were happy with flat prices, while big business loved the tax breaks, the import surcharges, and the price controls. All in a single weekend, Nixon had delivered them from union wage pressures, supplier price hikes, and foreign competition. The dollar ended 1971 at about $44 per ounce of gold. In gold terms, that is, America's trading partners, especially Japan, which had been holding large dollar balances, took a 25 percent loss on their holdings.

Although Nixon got his landslide, the cracks in the economy were too big to hide. The 1971 wage-and-price "90-day freeze," as it was originally billed, lasted for three years. Controls are always easier to put on than to take off. The underlying inflation builds to a point of explosiveness, and the inevitable thicket of rules offers profitable little crevices for the lucky or the well-connected. Organized labor stopped cooperating in 1974, but by then Nixon was deeply ensnared in the coils of Watergate. Congress forced the end of all controls in the spring, except for price controls on domestic oil. Removal of controls triggered double-digit inflation, the first since the 1940s, and the country suffered a nasty recession in 1974 and 1975. The decline of American competitiveness continued apace—in 1977, Chrysler averted bankruptcy only by dint of last-minute government loans.

THE DOLLAR EXPLOSION

The 1973 OPEC oil price hikes, which helped trigger the runaway inflation that marked the rest of the decade, were a direct consequence of floating the dollar. By 1973, when the OPEC countries tripled the price of oil, the dollar had fallen to about $100 per ounce of gold or about a third of its previous value. The Federal Reserve, however, kept printing dollars to match the ballooning import bills.

Oil was mostly priced in dollars, and most oil exporters had strong links with the United States and did their banking with the overseas branches of American banks. So American bank branches began to build large volumes of overseas deposits—the Eurodollars that had gotten a big push from Volcker's foreign securities tax. Economists began to fret over the challenge of "recycling the petrodollars," and the Ford administration expressly asked the banks to help.

The banks didn't need any advice. They were already relending their Eurodollar deposits to less-developed countries (LDCs) that had also been hard hit by the price increases. The favorites were Argentina and Mexico since they had large oil deposits to collateralize their debts, but Brazil was also on the favored list, mostly because it was big. "Big" was important: Banks opened overseas branches primarily to service their far-flung blue-chip American customers. They were not deep in lending and credit staff, and their petrodollar deposits were growing so fast they needed to place them wholesale. Since petrodollar loans were almost always guaranteed by the borrowing country governments, they could be classified as "sovereign debt," entitled to the highest risk rankings and requiring minimum credit work.

The petrodollar lending generated a vast upsurge in global liquidity. (If the Saudis take in $1 billion in oil revenues from America, and deposit it in an American bank, which lends it to Brazil, which buys another $1 billion in oil, which is deposited in an American bank and relent to . . . etc.) By 1982, Eurodollar balances had ballooned to a net $1 trillion, about a quarter of it tied up in LDC loans, with most of those—$176 billion—in just four countries: Mexico, Argentina, Brazil, and Venezuela. The money was supposed to be dedicated to revenue-producing projects, but enormous amounts were siphoned off into subsidies, current government spending, or sheer corruption.

Alarms from economists and central bankers were waved off, especially by Citibank's Walter Wriston. An official Citibank publication scoffed in 1981: "The concept of banks, flooded with OPEC deposits, chasing loans of deteriorating quality is an *Alice in Wonderland* fantasy."[6]

The most visible consequence of the flood of global dollars was a sharp increase in inflation, especially in the United States, where consumer prices rose at double-digit rates in the late 1970s—the only time in U.S. history that prices rose so fast. Kennedy's pro-growth economists had actually targeted a 2 percent inflation rate to speed growth. Keynesian demand management techniques, they were confident, would allow them to push the demand envelope but ratchet back whenever inflation broke out of a safe range. Inflation accelerated steadily, however, as Vietnam-related spending took off in 1966. By the time Lyndon Johnson left office, it was at 4.2 percent and rising, hitting 5.9 percent in 1970.

The real inflationary culprit, however, was Arthur Burns, Federal Reserve chairman under both Nixon and Gerald Ford. His stern lectures on monetary stability earned him the reputation as the nation's "number one inflation fighter." But inside the Fed, according to Fed historian William Greider, he was viewed as an "arrogant fraud."[7] It was Burns who gunned up the money supply to goose the economy in time for Nixon's 1972 campaign, and he opened the credit spigots after Jimmy Carter took office, allegedly in the hope of being reappointed.

The flood of dollars drove up the dollar price of gold—in effect, the dollar was becoming a debased currency. As far as the OPEC nations were concerned, the gold price of oil was actually lower by the end of the 1970s than it had been before their 1973 price increase. In self-defense, they tripled prices again in 1979. Since the dollar price of gold varied between $233 and $578 per ounce in 1979, OPEC was still losing ground in gold terms. The following year, when the dollar plunged as low as $850 an ounce, the gold price of oil was as low as it had ever been.

In the years immediately following the Camp David announcements, Volcker spent his time fruitlessly trying to work out a stable set of monetary relations with America's largest trading partners. As hopes for a new framework faded, he resigned from the Treasury in 1974, intending to return to banking. Arthur Burns, however, persuaded him to take the job of chairman of the New York Federal Reserve Bank, the most important of the twelve district federal reserve banks, for it was a key point of contact between the federal monetary apparatus and Wall Street and international money markets. After a brief stint at Princeton University in 1975, he served at the New York Fed until 1979.

By that time, it was clear that the United States had lost control of its economy, and made a complete mess of its international monetary responsibilities. Volcker was summoned back to Washington as chairman of the Federal Reserve Board, with a mandate to fix the problem.

VOLCKER QUELLS INFLATION

President Jimmy Carter made no secret that Volcker was his third or fourth choice for the Fed chairmanship. Volcker probably increased the president's unease by stressing the importance of a politically independent Fed chairman in his only pre-appointment interview. Stuart Eizenstat, Carter's domestic policy adviser, later said that "Volcker was selected because he was the candidate of Wall Street. This was their price."[8] Volcker's assignment, in short, was to restore order, in whatever way he saw fit.

When Volcker's appointment was confirmed in August, inflation was increasing about 1 percent a month. Some leftish economists thought that might be okay. Around the world, a number of high-inflation countries had been experimenting with "indexing"—all prices and paychecks could be regularly adjusted for measured inflation. The bookkeeping was awkward, but computers could handle it.

More important, the costs of reducing inflation looked unacceptable. Economists had spent a half century exploring the trade-off between employment and inflation, known as the "Phillips curve," and research suggested that the trade-off costs were *very* high. "Okun's law," named after former Council of Economic Advisers chairman Arthur Okun, stipulated that every 1 percent of inflation reduction would cost a 3 percent reduction in employment, and a 9 *percent* reduction in GDP! No traditional Democrat could enlist in an inflation war on those terms.[9]

But Volcker's job was to reassure the world financial community, not Keynesian academics. (In fact, Okun's law was just wrong; it's perfectly possible to have low inflation and high employment.) Inflation fears were traumatizing long-term investors, siphoning money away from the bonds and stocks that financed business productivity and fueling "hard" asset bubbles in gold, art, and real estate. And the world economy was still denominated in dollars. If the dollar went the way of the peso, other nations would adjust, but it could take years. On spot markets, the dollar price of oil was going up 6 percent a month; gold had jumped 28 percent in a single month. A Weimar-type hyperinflation, and a cataclysmic crash, weren't inconceivable. Several times during the 1979–1982 period, the bankers and economists who gathered each month for the policy-setting Federal Open Market Committee (FOMC) meetings in the boardroom of the Federal Reserve talked seriously about the dangers of another "1929" or "1931."[10] People were that afraid.

But no Fed chairman is completely independent, not even Volcker, who assumed office with an unusual degree of policy-making freedom. All important policy decisions are made by the FOMC—which comprises the seven members of the Federal Reserve Board, plus the president of the New York Federal Reserve Bank, and, on a rotating basis, four of the other eleven presidents of district Federal Reserve banks. Since financial markets hate split votes on matters of importance, Fed chairmen typically go to great lengths to ensure unanimity or close to it. The chairman must also watch his political flanks. A president can attack him for damaging the economy, and congressmen can drag him through endless hearings. Not even the crustiest of chairmen, like Volcker, enjoy being vilified in public.

When he took office, Volcker especially could not ignore the newly empowered monetarists, anointed the soothsayers *du jour* of political economy. If inflation always arose from an excess of money, as Milton Friedman taught, then the surest way to reduce it was to reduce the supply of money. The supply of money was equal to the stock of money—"M1" or cash and checking accounts—times its turnover rate or "velocity." Since velocity was roughly constant over long periods of time—or so Friedman claimed—the Federal Reserve could achieve stable prices simply by ensuring that M1 growth approximated the rate of growth in the real economy.* Wall Street was an enthusiastic convert.

---

* The stability of velocity was wishful thinking on Friedman's part, reflecting his strong interest in shrinking government. A simple policy rule of increasing the money supply at the same rate as growth in the real economy could, in principle, reduce Fed policy to a simple algorithm.

Neither Volcker nor most of his fellow FOMC members were Friedmanites, preferring the traditional Fed tools of manipulating short-term interest rates—primarily the "Fed Funds Rate," the rate that federal reserve banks charged each other for loans of free reserves—by contracting or expanding bank reserves. (If the Fed starts buying up treasury paper held by the public, it would increase the public's, and the banking system's, holdings of cash, and vice versa.)

In theory, since bank lending, or credit creation, is the primary driver of the money supply,* changes in Fed Funds, bank reserves, and M1 should move up and down in a fairly predictable relationship. But in real life, they don't. American credit markets are a heaving ocean, and the Fed is just a tributary sluice gate at a distant shore. Events at the sluice gate may be transmitted through the ocean, but are so swamped by ambient noise that it's impossible to track their effects. Experience has taught that there is no reason to expect a tight linkage between money-supply measures, and rates and reserves. Over quite extended periods, in fact, they can give entirely different signals. Given a choice of imprecise tools, experienced Fed hands usually preferred to send public signals with interest rates, because they were the most easily understood by businessmen.

The standard story of Volcker's victory over inflation is that he achieved it by a firm application of monetarist principles. Since he

---

* Assume I have $1000 in a checking account. The bank is free to lend that amount, less a reserve to cover possible withdrawals, to a third party. Assume the bank lends $500, which the borrower also deposits into a checking account. Total checking account money is now $1500. Since checking account money is the major component of M1, dampening or stimulating bank lending will have a commensurate effect on M1.

had never been known as a monetarist, I asked him, some forty years later, about his apparent conversion. There is "certainly some truth in the monetarist position," he said, "and I found it useful, both as a way to explain what we were doing, and as a way to discipline ourselves."[11]

I take that as a permissible diplomatic fib. FOMC transcripts from this period suggest that his conversion, and that of most of the other members, was a bit like the Christianity of *converso* Jews in Inquisition-era Spain.* Shortly after his appointment, for example, after the FOMC had agreed to tighten the Fed Funds Rate, Volcker said:

> [W]e also have to show some resistance to the growth in money. I would note that that remains a source of political support for us. It's not every day that we get a letter from the leader of the Black Caucus [in the House] exhorting us to show more restraint on the money supply side. So I'm going to carry that letter close to my heart, whatever we decide today.[12]

The pressure for monetarist orthodoxy grew even more intense once the avowedly monetarist Reagan administration took office. At an FOMC meeting a few weeks after the inauguration, Lawrence Roos, the president of the St. Louis Fed, and perhaps the Committee's purest Friedmanite, warned: "People in the Ad-

---

* William Greider's well-known history of the Fed takes Volcker to task for his "rigid monetarist approach." But Greider did not have access to the FOMC transcripts. (Alan Greenspan apparently told him that they didn't exist.)

ministration . . . are going to watch us like a hawk [on adherence to monetarism], and we're not going to be able to bluff our way through this."[13]

Volcker's other intensely scrutinizing audiences were the ministries of finance and central banks of the major industrial countries. When Volcker attended a meeting of central bankers in Belgrade in October 1979, he found himself sharply taken to task by his peers, especially by the German Bundesbank. Volcker had taken a strong anti-inflation stance at his confirmation hearing and pointedly raised rates at his very first FOMC meeting. But at the September meeting, with the economy seeming to head toward recession, the FOMC adopted a steady-as-she-goes stance, but only by a split vote. Analysts read it as wavering on inflation.

The negative reaction from his fellow central bankers was so strong that Volcker cut short his trip, and called an emergency FOMC meeting for October 6. Briefing the committee, Volcker said that the overseas ministries were "very nervous," and the "the discussions abroad were very difficult." Markets were "very volatile," and he had been taken aback by "the depths of the feelings" among his peers. Even though the transcript was confidential, he insisted that the tape be turned off when he discussed the particulars of what was said.

To make a dramatic demonstration of the Fed's commitment, Volcker said he was thinking of formally adopting monetarist orthodoxy on the money supply. He didn't pretend that he had been converted. But he thought that "by changing psychology a bit, we might actually get more bang for the buck. . . . I am not saying that that reasoning is correct but I think it is the reasoning in the market psychologically."

But he warned the committee:

> [W]e may get locked into a technique that isn't very suitable
> over the longer run, including into 1980. The technique
> might have implications for interest rates or other things that
> we wouldn't be happy about in other situations, yet it would
> be hard to reverse our ground. I think that we also have to
> consider the risk of putting a lot more emphasis now on the
> money supply targets knowing that there is no technique
> that's going to assure that we are going to achieve [them]. . . .
> We could well end up exceeding the targets for the year,
> after making a hullabaloo about this change in technique.[14]

Volcker carried the vote and held an unusual evening press
conference to announce the new policies. Short-term interest rates
were being reset to 13.5 percent, then the highest level in history,
and new lending restrictions would be imposed on banks. Most
prominently, however, Volcker announced the policy shift toward
strict monetarism; inflation would be brought down by tight control
over money. If he was looking for shock effect, he got it. Amid a
sharp sell-off on Wall Street, the *New York Times* editorialized
under the headline, "Mr. Volcker's Verdun":

> When the chairman of the Federal Reserve, Paul Volcker,
> talks, Wall Street listens. That, so far, is the only conclusion
> to be drawn from the turmoil in financial markets that fol-
> lowed the Fed's [announcements]. . . . It will take months to
> find out whether Mr. Volcker's shock treatment will dispel
> American expectations about inflation or simply make an al-
> ready depressing condition even worse. The odds, unfortu-

nately, are against Mr. Volcker. . . . Mr. Volcker is a gambler.
He is betting high, with a poor hand. The entire nation
needs to hope that he beats the odds.[15]

Volcker did break the back of inflation. Contrary to the conventional story, he didn't do it by cracking down on money—although he made a sporting try, all his fears of the risks from a
monetarist focus came true. Over the next three years, he took the
country on a wild ride.

The first few months of the Fed's monetarist experiment, in
terms of appearances at least, went fairly well. The money-supply
numbers behaved the way Volcker said they would, although the
staff conceded that they had been "fairly lucky in coming up with
growth in money that was pretty consistent with what the Committee wanted."[16]

But the outcomes in the real economy were dreadful. Despite
slow monetary growth, and Fed Funds at 13.5 to 14 percent through
the fall, inflation actually accelerated, driven by a stiff OPEC price
increase. January inflation ran at an 18 percent annual rate, consumer spending was rising even faster, and foreigners kept dumping
dollars. The Fed staff forecast negative 2.2 percent inflation-adjusted
growth for 1980, which would have been the worst year since
1946, a year of mass military demobilization.

Then the money numbers, which Wall Street tracked like a
pulse rate, went haywire. Weirdly, free-market monetarists somehow hadn't guessed that if the Fed cracked down on conventional
money stock, profit-seeking banks would create new financial
techniques to avoid the restrictions. Which they promptly did—
spinning out high-yielding money market mutual funds, interest-
bearing checking accounts, electronic sweeps to marshal corporate

cash, and much more.* For the next year and a half, each month's discussion of the monetary figures at the FOMC had an air of semi-comic desperation—how could the Fed shift the definitions of "money" so they would look on track without creating suspicion of its monetarist bona fides?

By May 1980, they were trapped. For some reason, the money-supply numbers were in free fall and interest rates were dropping, while the real economy and inflation were both roaring ahead. Monetarist doctrine said that it was time to expand bank reserves, regardless of what else was going on. Every traditionalist instinct said that was crazy—like pouring gasoline on the inflation bonfire. The committee, in other words, was in precisely the box Volcker had warned of the previous October. In fact, it turned out the drop in the money supply was real, but it was a temporary reaction to a Carter administration clampdown on consumer credit, plus an emotional appeal from the president asking the public to tear up their credit cards. (Tens of thousands of people mailed their cut-up credit cards to the White House.) The FOMC members, of course, had some inkling that the credit controls might have caused the sudden shift in the monetary data, but it was too soon to know for sure, and no one suspected that the impact could be so large.

---

* At the time, I was working at a money center bank as the executive responsible for corporate banking products. Our hottest offering was cash management—for example, building a nationwide electronic collection system so a beer company could collect from its distributors on the day of delivery. It dawned on me that we were increasing the velocity of money, thereby invalidating the basic assumptions of the Fed's October 1979 policy shift.

Some samples of the debate:

> Mr. Roos [committed monetarist]: A lot of people in the real world [at least] in the real world where I live are hoping desperately that when this incompatibility occurs we will do what we said we were going to do: Keep an eye on the [money supply] targets and let interest rates fluctuate. . . .
>
> Mr. Wallich [traditionalist]: This is attributing to the money supply a significance that I see hardly any economists attributing to it. The money supply is a means of getting [desired] interest rates.
>
> Mr. Partee [committed monetarist]: Well, we've announced our targets to the Congress not in terms of interest rates but in terms of [monetary] aggregates. We've never mentioned interest rates in our targets to Congress. . . .
>
> Mr. Schultz [traditionalist]: I am amazed, and I must admit disturbed, at the fact that I haven't heard the word inflation mentioned around this table this morning. My word, it was only two months ago that we were wild about the subject. . . . There aren't very many people around the country who understand our change from a federal funds [interest rate] operating target to a reserves [money supply] operating target. But a lot of people understand that what the Fed does is crucial in the fight against inflation . . . [and easing money supply could accelerate inflation.][17]

The committee voted 10–2 to swallow their doubts, stick with monetarism, and expand reserves. The two "No" votes, ironically, came from Roos and Partee, the dedicated monetarists—presumably because the FOMC didn't push down the monetary aggregates as fast as true doctrine suggested; and because the board had reserved the right to intervene if interest rates fluctuated too much, which to monetarists, missed the whole point. As Roos repeatedly argued, monetarists focus on money and let interest rates fall where they may.

The new policy was a disaster. Interest rates dropped like a stone, the economy leaped from zero growth to an amazing 7.6 percent real growth in the fourth quarter, and inflation shot back up to double-digit levels. The message to the world was that the Fed had lost control. For much of the late fall and early winter, Volcker effectively went on the political stump—making congressional appearances, giving speeches, and issuing press releases in an effort to restore credibility to his war on inflation.

An extended FOMC discussion the following winter suggests that all but the committee's few diehards understood the Heisenberg-like trap they were in. By pegging policy to a single variable—the money supply—you changed the nature of the variable. As the staff explained, if money growth were tightly managed, interest rates would be highly volatile; conversely, if rates were tightly managed, the volatility would shift to the money numbers. One member said, "I think 1981 is going to be a year when none of us has the faintest idea what M1 really means."[18]

As a practical matter, while the FOMC maintained its monetarist rhetoric, Volcker shifted the committee's focus back to squeezing interest rates. By January 1981, Fed Funds were at an unheard-of 19 percent, while 3-month treasury bills were paying 20 percent. The blistering growth rate from the last quarter of 1980 carried over into the first quarter of 1981, but the economy slipped into a recession over the rest of the year. As the Fed's grim tightening continued in the teeth of a deeper and deeper recession, howls of protest rose in Congress. To his credit, Reagan made a ringing statement of support in April: "I have confidence in the announced policies of the Federal Reserve board. . . . [N]either this administration nor the Federal Reserve will allow a return to the fiscal and monetary policies of the past that have created the current conditions."[19]

The drop in the economy in 1982 was a negative 1.9 percent, the worst in the postwar era. The unemployment rate, which had been 5.8 percent in 1979, jumped to 9.7 percent, and would have been higher if not for an unusually large number of labor force withdrawals. Inflation slowed a tad, but stayed stuck in double digits.

To an amazing degree, people put up with it. One of the district Fed presidents reported at a spring 1982 FOMC meeting that both business executives and labor leaders in his region "were feeling very severe recessionary pressures," but "recognized that it was part of the process of bringing down inflation." "[E]ven from the labor group," he said, "there was a strong recognition, and hope really, that we will continue to look to solving the long-term fundamental problem rather than reacting to the pain of the moment."[20] At about the same time, Volcker accepted an invitation to speak to the annual convention of the home builders' association—with some trepidation, since they were one of the hardest-hit of all industry sectors. Volcker's message was uncompromising: "We would all like to see recovery . . . [but it is] even more crucial that growth be sustainable for years ahead. . . . [If] we let up on our anti-inflation effort . . . the pain we have suffered would have been for naught—and we would only be putting off to some later time an even more painful day of reckoning." To his surprise, he got a standing ovation.[21]

By mid-1982, however, nervousness over continued high rates dominated the FOMC discussions. Volcker discreetly let it be known that he would not let the Fed Funds Rate rise above 15 percent, regardless of money-supply data. The *New York Times* called it a sign of the "new pragmatism,"[22] and over the next few months, it became widely understood that the monetarist experiment was over—money-supply data had informational value, but the economic consequences of manipulating the money stock were too imprecise to make it a useful policy tool. Inflation—blessedly—broke sometime mid-year, and growth in the consumer price index (CPI) during the second half of the year was essentially flat. By year-end, Fed Funds were down to a reasonable 8.7 percent. Growth was barely positive in the fourth quarter, but turned in a respectable 4.5 percent in 1983, and a booming 7.2 percent in 1984. The dollar soared.

There was one more test. After growth took off like a rocket in 1983, it stayed quite high through the first half of 1984, rekindling Wall Street's inflation fears. Volcker was convinced that too fast a recovery could retrigger inflationary impetus. The administration, worried about the election, at first exerted strong pressure to maintain the easing, with considerable support within the Fed, both from Democrats who wanted more growth and Republicans who wanted a second Reagan term. Volcker held firm and raised interest rates in July; luckily, he slowed growth without actually choking it off. Once again, Reagan made a strong statement of support. Real GDP for the year, despite the second half slowdown, was still a blistering 7.2 percent, but the inflation rate continued to fall.

GDP in 1985 was a respectable 4.1 percent, while the inflation rate dropped to only 1.9 percent, a twenty-year low. Wall Street was finally convinced: The interest rate on long-term treasury bonds dropped, and with only mild interruptions, continued to fall for the next twenty years.

Volcker had put the country through the wringer. But the grim, and dramatic, demonstration that America would endure a major increase in unemployment and a very deep recession to break inflation transformed the world's impression of American economic management. From that point, America's commitment to price stability was assumed as a matter of course.

When Volcker resigned from the Fed in 1987, breaking the cycle of inflation was his singular bequest to the country. That legacy, won with so much blood and sweat, was avidly drawn down for the next twenty years. It was only the faith of a credulous world in the fundamental responsibility and stability of the United States that allowed the creation of the mountainous financial imbalances that went into full avalanche mode in late 2007.

VOLCKER AND THE BANKS

Although the inflation battles are the best-remembered episodes from Volcker's Fed chairmanship, he also had to manage through a host of problems with banks, most notably the LDC loan crisis that finally came to a head in 1982.[23] In many ways, it was a foreshadowing of the credit crunch of the 2000s. Many of the institutional players, like Citigroup (then Citibank), are the same, both in name and in arrogance, having peremptorily brushed aside warnings from regulators throughout the 1970s.

The attraction of the LDC business for the banks was much the same as those of the high-flying businesses of the 2000s—a half dozen or so big U.S. money-center banks made very large fees by packaging up mega-loans to developing countries, especially in Latin America, and then syndicating them throughout the banking system. One of the government's problems in resolving the crisis was that the bad loans were marbled through the entire country—even small local banks proudly sported their piece of the big-league loan they had been privileged to purchase from Chase or Citi.

And the business process was every bit as reckless. Poor countries, struggling to attain middle-class status, were awarded tens of billions in loans, denominated in dollars, at floating interest rates, which were rising sharply in the inflationary 1970s. When they couldn't pay, the loans were rolled over, now including the unpaid interest, and then rolled over again. By 1982, the tens of billions of loans made in the mid-1970s had ballooned into $327 billion in Latin American dollar debts—almost all in Mexico, Brazil, and Argentina. Scheduled rollovers would drive the totals over the half-trillion mark, or nearly their combined GDPs, within just a couple more years.

The LDC loans, finally, were deeply entwined with the American adventures in inflation. The ocean of dollars sloshing around the world undercut American claims to fiscal probity, trashed the dollar's value in gold terms, and drove the relentless upward climb in oil and other commodity prices. Conversely, as Volcker started to ratchet up American interest rates, the floating-rate coupons on the American loans became impossibly high, eliminating even the most wistful pretense that they might be repaid.

Widespread LDC defaults virtually assured insolvency for the biggest American banks. Even though they had aggressively sold off their loans, in 1982 the eight largest American banks still retained almost $60 billion on their own books, accounting for a sixth of their total loan book and about $2\frac{1}{2}$ times their capital. In short, they were dead in the water.

The crisis came to a head in 1982, when Mexico defaulted on a payment—packaging its default announcement with a demand for a much bigger loan. Volcker fumed at an FOMC meeting about "a decade of loose practices":

> Sooner or later Mexico was going to get into trouble. They borrowed $20 billion last year. And they borrowed heaven knows how many billions in dollars net this year when they could still borrow—before they got in trouble. . . . But I think it's patently obvious that Mexico was going to borrow all it could borrow and all the banks were going to give them and at some point that was going to come to an end. And it was going to be a crisis situation.[24]

He might be forgiven for sounding grumpy. He had just completed three years at the helm of the Fed, and the LDC loan crisis would be his *fourth* bank bailout. In 1980, he had spent weeks arranging a $1 billion–plus bailout for the consortium of banks that had stupidly financed an attempted silver corner by Nelson and Bunker Hunt, two bachelor oil tycoons known for their nastiness. The next year, New York banks, especially Chase, let an obscure government securities dealer, Drysdale Securities, run up an untenable $4 billion position that could have brought down Street firms like tenpins. A strenuous intervention by Volcker forced Chase and a few other banks to eat the losses—$250 million in the case of Chase.

A month after that, it was revealed that a storefront bank in Oklahoma, Penn Square, had run up a $2 billion portfolio of dicey oil loans, which it off-loaded by syndicating them to bigger banks— half to Continental Illinois, then the fourth largest bank in the country, and the second largest share to Chase. With oil prices falling, the portfolio was nearly worthless. Penn Square was shut down at a federal cost of more than $300 million in insurance payoffs, while Continental Illinois staggered on until it went into federal receivership in 1984.

Those problems, of course, were dwarfed by the LDC crisis. Volcker reviewed the challenges for a fall 1982 FOMC meeting: Mexico was in a "very difficult political transition" with $100 billion in external debt, and "I don't think anybody can bank a lot of money on that particular situation." Argentina was "unable to finance its needs in the markets and is in substantial arrears on its indebtedness." Ecuador was "facing an inability to service its debt in a matter of weeks." Chile was "unable to finance itself at the moment and rapidly depleting its reserves." Bolivia was "basically in default" as were Costa Rica and Peru. Even the "strong" countries like Brazil, which was trying hard to maintain sound practices, had been unable to control its indebtedness. Fed surveys also showed that an "astonishing" number of small-and medium-sized banks were involved in LDC lending, mostly through buying loan participations from the big guys.

Volcker wound up a decidedly gloomy *tour d'horizon*:

I'd say that all this leads to a considerable feeling in financial markets and elsewhere of developing disarray, a certain floundering . . . which feeds upon itself. . . . There is not a single source of real strength or certainty out there. . . . Extraordinary things may have to be done. We haven't had a parallel to this situation historically except to the extent 1929 was a parallel.[25]

The LDC crisis dragged on for the rest of the decade. Although the federal government did not bail out the at-risk banks, the regulators engaged in a conspiracy of silence—"forbearance," as it was officially called—treating LDC loans as if they were full-value assets, so the banks could pretend to be solvent, while they slowly rebuilt their capital and reserves. Bank profitability and share prices were depressed over most of the period. Latin American countries were in deep recession in 1982 and 1983, and managed only a bit more than 2 percent growth for the rest of the decade, or less than population growth. In other words, they got a lot poorer.

The clouds didn't completely lift until 1989, when the new administration of George H. W. Bush floated the "Brady Plan," named after Nicholas Brady, a holdover from the Reagan administration at Treasury. "Brady bonds" were an ingenious set of tradable new securities, backed by deeply discounted treasuries, that allowed both borrowing countries and banks to get the loans off their books. They were completely successful and never cost the American taxpayer a dime.

The most striking aspect in all these episodes is how boldly the bankers walked into one abyss after another. Financing the Hunts'

attempt to corner the world silver market is the antithesis of intel-
ligent banking. In the Drysdale and Penn Square instances, the
chase for profits overrode even rudimentary checking on what the
borrowers were doing with the money.

In the LDC case, especially, regulators were severely criticized
for being asleep at the switch. But they had started raising caution
flags in the mid-1970s, and Volcker expressed his concerns directly
to Walter Wriston, chairman of Citibank and one of the biggest
LDC players, in 1980. Wriston reportedly told him: "Mr. Chairman, I totally disagree with you. These international loans are the
best loans I've got. I've had few defaults on them and my profit
margin is very good."[26] (More or less the same line that Citigroup's
Chuck Prince was peddling in 2007.) If the regulators had started
forcing write-downs of the LDC loans early in the process, as
they should have done, Wriston and his fellow executives would
have screamed bloody murder, and Congress would have backed
them.

The performance of market analysts and rating agencies was
especially dismal. Right up to the Penn Square crisis, Continental
Illinois was lauded as "one of the finest money-center banks going."
Money-center bank bond issues generally carried the highest rat-
ings, with hardly a twitch of concern until the LDC crisis exploded
onto the financial pages. If the raters didn't see the banks' growing
dependence on just a handful of high-risk borrowers, they could
have just asked the feds.

A career like Volcker's creates a worldview thoroughly vaccinated
against nostrums and dogmas. Listening to Walter Wriston declaim
on the quality of LDC loans. Hearing academic Keynesians insist
that they can control inflation. Watching a different crew of aca-

demics explain how unregulated markets minimize risk. Or seeing how predictably politicians demand faster growth in election years.

When you talk to Volcker, or listen to his speeches, you hear a distillation of a quarter-century's lore from the center of economic policy. Use common sense. Watch out for imbalances. Choose moderate growth over fast growth—it lasts longer, and doesn't end in catastrophe. Beware of economists who believe in their models. Have faith in markets, but don't trust Wall Street. Never rely on advice from people who get rich by risking other people's money. Accept that there are financiers who don't need regulatory oversight (but they're all dead).

FOREBODINGS

The irresponsible behavior of the banks was a symptom of deep changes at work in financial markets. George Soros had anticipated most of them in his 1972 memo on "Growth Banking." Traditionally, lending in the United States had fallen into three institutional buckets. Residential mortgages were sourced and serviced by local savings and loans (S&Ls). Business lending came mostly from banks; the bread-and-butter business loan was the working-capital line that was usually negotiated annually, with drawdowns fluctuating with a company's sales and collections cycle. Long-term lending, like commercial mortgages or industrial project finance, were placed with insurance companies or financed in the bond market.

Those categories were breaking down in the 1970s. Unstable interest rates were destroying the S&Ls. (S&Ls were funding long-term fixed-rate mortgages with short-term deposits. If deposit rates bounced higher than their book of mortgage rates, they were insolvent.*) Wall Street investment banks were picking off the most profitable business banking products. Why was IBM paying bank interest for working capital? It could borrow more cheaply on its own name. So Wall Street invented "commercial paper." Even with a small underwriting fee attached, a Merrill or a Morgan Stanley would create a capital line for IBM, and finance it by selling IBM paper. Rubbing it in, the banks were reduced to supplying credit lines to the investment banks at razor-thin fees to support their new commercial paper businesses.

It took a while, but the banks struck back. Most of the investment firms were still partnerships, without the deep pools of equity capital that the commercial banks had. Investment bankers were smarter and had nicer shirts, but corporate advice sometimes went down better when it came with locked-in funding. Starting in the late 1980s, the banks chipped away at the old Glass-Steagall walls, until full establishment of the "bank holding company" in 1999.

But two could play at that game. One by one the big investment banks went public—Merrill, Goldman, Bear, Lehman, Morgan Stanley. The capital poured in. Goldman may have been the first public company to make the lion's share of its revenues and profits from "principal transactions"—betting the house's own money. Everyone else jumped into the pool. But they weren't really "principal" transactions. When old J. P. Morgan engaged in principal transactions, he was betting his and his partners' *personal* money.

---

* The government "solved" that problem by setting a maximum deposit rate. But when rate disparities became very wide, consumers began putting their money into other instruments, like the burgeoning new "money market mutual funds."

The new generation of principal transactions were really "share-holder" transactions. The firm execs just got the upside.

Finance became much more of a quicksilver enterprise—creating and trading financial instruments in place of long-term credit provision and monitoring. Time-honored modes of behavior—traditional safety rules that regulators took for granted—went by the boards. Financial sector liquidity and profits steadily rose, as did leverage and risk. The changes propagated slowly for a decade or more until a flexion point was passed, and there was the sudden explosion of risk that has marked the 2000s.

Volcker retired from the Fed in 1987 at the expiration of his second term as chairman. Relations with the Reagan administration were fraying. Treasury Secretary James Baker was pushing for easier money and faster growth than Volcker felt was safe. He agreed with Baker that a rate reduction was not unreasonable, but he wanted to do it in concert with other major currencies to avoid triggering a run on the dollar. There was an extraordinarily testy moment in February 1986, when Preston Martin, a Reagan loyalist who had been installed as vice chairman, and three other Reagan appointees outvoted Volcker in an unscheduled vote to lower the discount rate. Volcker was outraged. "It was obviously preconceived," he told an interviewer. "Nobody had ever called for a vote suddenly against a chairman when it wasn't even on the agenda."[27] Volcker succeeded in reversing the vote—it was undoubtedly a resignation issue, which would have shocked global currency markets. Two weeks later, he acquiesced to the rate cut, but by that time, Japan and Germany had agreed to simultaneous cuts, so the dollar was not unduly exposed.

Volcker's second term as chairman ended in 1987. The administration made a show of offering him another term: Volcker understood that they didn't mean it, and he wouldn't have accepted if they had.

AFTER THE FED

When Volcker retired from the Fed, he received multiple offers to join a major bank or Wall Street firm but was cautious about becoming a highly paid figurehead or government door-opener. Instead he joined James D. Wolfensohn and Company, a new boutique investment bank. Jim Wolfensohn, the founder, was an Australian who had been a rainmaking investment banker at Salomon. His new firm was intended as a low-key traditional advisory firm, with long-term client relationships and no underwriting or other market-making activities. It was perfect for Volcker. The pay, while modest by Wall Street standards, was a great financial relief after years of shuttling between New York and Washington on a government paycheck. He joined as chairman but was active in the firm's business, becoming managing partner—effectively, the CEO—when Wolfensohn was appointed president of the World Bank in 1995. By then, the firm's size had tripled to 140 employees and ten partners. In 1996, it was sold to Bankers Trust, and Volcker, pushing seventy, started a third career as global financial statesman.

The primary "brand" that Volcker carried into his post-Wolfensohn career wasn't that of the investment banker or international financial sage, although he qualified on both counts. The real Volcker brand, outweighing all his financial accomplishments, was his reputation for rock-solid integrity and utter incorruptibility. If a major company or an international organization had a credibility or corruption problem that it wanted to fix, one way was to induce Paul Volcker to head up an investigative committee. The downside was that he took his reputation very seriously. He would dig deeply and call the shots as he saw them, and the results could be embarrassing.

Three high-profile assignments epitomize Volcker's career as an integrity doctor. The first, in 1996, he took only at the ardent request of a Swiss banker friend. The assignment was to lead an inquiry into the Holocaust-era Jewish bank accounts allegedly in suspension in Swiss banks since World War II. In the 1930s and 1940s, many German Jews, afraid of having their assets expropriated by the Nazis, moved their money to Switzerland. Many of the depositors, inevitably, died at the hands of the Nazis. But instead of trying to track down the owners or heirs of long-dormant accounts, Swiss banks simply sat on them for the next half century, benefiting from the free use of the cash.

The inquiry played out like a Monty Python skit. At first, the Swiss insisted that they had fully investigated the possible existence of Nazi-era Jewish accounts in 1962 and found only a very few, which they had transferred to the decedents' estates or to charities. Under Volcker's cold eye, they looked again and found another thousand accounts with $40 million in assets. And then they looked a little harder, and found perhaps 15,000 to 20,000 such accounts, or maybe even 54,000. . . . [28]

There were other pressures on the Swiss—a major international lawsuit, and rumblings in the U.S. Congress about making life more difficult for the secretive banks. But Volcker has a unique talent for concentrating minds, and since he commands wide-spectrum trust, a settlement mechanism that he endorses as "fair" will be widely accepted as such, because it usually is.

A second inquiry was more daunting. That was the inquiry into corruption in the United Nations' Oil for Food Program that operated from 1996 through 2003. After the 1991 Gulf War, Saddam Hussein's Iraq was a pariah nation that most western nations refused to trade with. The trade embargo, however, worked dreadful hardship on the Iraqi people, and stories spread of large-scale malnutrition and retarded development among Iraqi children.

The western powers therefore agreed to allow Iraq to sell limited amounts of oil to the West, provided that the proceeds were spent for humanitarian purposes, like infant formula, foodstuffs, vitamins, medications, and similar goods. The management of Oil for Food was assigned to the UN. Oil purchasing contracts from Iraq were put out to bid and the funds were deposited at the UN. In cooperation with Iraqi officials who advised on need levels, the funds were used to purchase humanitarian supplies, which were also contracted on the basis of competitive bids.

The amounts of money involved were very large, some $64 billion over the entire seven years. Allegations of corruption and kickbacks swirled from the very start, feeding into American conservatives' generalized distaste for international organizations of all kinds. When corruption allegations were raised about Kojo Annan, the son of Kofi Annan, the UN Secretary-General, Annan senior asked for a full investigation. An investigative committee was empanelled in April 2004, inevitably chaired by Volcker. (American conservatives argued there was a conflict of interest, since he was a director of the American United Nations Association, a pro-UN citizens' group.)

There was no whitewash. Volcker's IIC (Independent Inquiry Committee) worked for almost two years, with Volcker himself virtually on a full-time basis. They plowed through thousands of pages of documents, most of which had to be reconstructed from chaotic files, and they published an extended series of reports that ran to well over 1,000 pages laying out the full extent of the graft.

In brief, the Iraqis managed to skim $1.8 billion from the Oil for Food program. The smallest share, perhaps surprisingly, came from the oil contracts. In all, the Iraqis sold $64 billion of oil, and exacted illegal surcharges of $229 million. The lion's share of the graft was in the purchases of humanitarian goods. Of the 3,600 companies participating in the program, 2,300 made illegal payments to the Iraqis, usually in the form of fake "service" and "transportation" fees. On the Iraqi side, almost all of the money flowed to the regime, although various UN officials who facilitated the graft received substantial payments as well—and did their best to obstruct the investigations. The committee was sharply critical of Kofi Annan's son, who concealed his employment by an important inspection contractor and did not cooperate with the inquiry. While Kofi Annan himself claimed to have been "exonerated" by the report, in fact the committee concluded only that there was "insufficient evidence" to tie the senior Annan to his son's involvement or to refute the son's claim that his father was in the dark about his activities.

The IIC also produced a stream of additional reports on program management and results. The mismanagement at the UN was appalling, and the committee rather wearily produced a long list of reform recommendations, while acknowledging that outsiders had been producing such lists for years. The good news was that the actual results of the program, while doubtless far less than they should have been, were substantially positive. On a series of health and quality-of-life issues, Iraqis were clearly better off as a result of the program. Measures of child malnutrition and stunting; of disease prevalence, such as cholera and diarrhea, associated with damaged water infrastructure; and of the availability of basic medicines all improved substantially, in some cases returning to their 1991 levels.[29] Unsatisfying as some of the inquiry's results were, all in all, the committee discharged a gnarly task about as fairly and as thoroughly as it was possible to expect.

Volcker's third high-profile independent committee chairmanship was to review and make recommendations on the internal anticorruption mechanisms at the World Bank, as part of then president Paul Wolfowitz's drive to reduce corruption in field project financing. The committee's job was complicated by Wolfowitz's resignation while its work was still in progress. Wolfowitz had been unpopular among the staff, and his resignation was prompted in part by allegations that he had shown favoritism toward his companion, who was also an employee. The inquiry committee seems to have been as unpopular within the Bank as Wolfowitz himself.

The assignment was a thankless one, but it was important. World Bank annual development spending is in the $24 to $25 billion range, which represents about a quarter of global development spending. Ben Heineman, former GE vice president and general counsel, served on the committee. He told me that Volcker went about the assignment very seriously and diligently. He was "extraordinarily concerned about due process," Heineman said, "very careful, in a very good way, very statesmanlike, and very gracious in leading the panel and the staff." The committee's narrow terms of reference was to lay out the mission for the internal anticorruption function. The proposed new vision was set out in a seven-page introduction to the final report. "Paul basically wrote that himself," Heineman said, "and was very proud of it."[30]

Even when he is not chairing investigative committees, Volcker has plenty to occupy himself. He is chairman of the Group of Thirty, an advisory council composed of some of the world's leading financial experts and economists, and a founding member of the Trilateral Commission; he sits on several corporate boards; he is a much sought-after speaker; and he has had several part-time academic stints. More recently, he has been prominently involved both in the campaign and the new presidency of Barack Obama.

ENDORSING CHANGE

Volcker watchers have long known that he strongly disagreed with the laissez-faire regulatory attitude adopted by Alan Greenspan, his successor at the Federal Reserve. But as a man of the old school, a throwback to an era when it was improper to criticize your successor, he maintained silence.

As the economy continued to perform unusually well into the 1990s—the "Great Moderation," as it was sometimes called—Greenspan achieved the status of senior guru, or Maestro, as Bob Woodward dubbed him. For Greenspan's admirers, and for

Greenspan himself, the apparent good performance of the economy was final confirmation of his antiregulatory zealotry, which took on the status of sacred dogma. The consequence of peering at the economy through doctrinaire lenses was that Greenspan badly missed the thunderheads building by 2004 or so, until the hurricane struck. At least Greenspan had the grace to admit as much to a congressional committee. ("Those of us who have looked to the self-interest of lending institutions to protect shareholders' equity, myself included, are in a state of shocked disbelief."[31]) Few of his acolytes, who still dominate Wall Street, have made similar admissions.

Volcker finally broke his silence in April 2008 in a blistering speech at the Economic Club of New York. It is worth quoting at length. He began by speaking of the mid-1970s financial crisis in New York City, the last time he had addressed the club. He went on:

> Until the New York crisis, the country had been free from any sense of financial crisis for more than 40 years. In contrast, today's financial crisis is the culmination, as I count them, of at least five serious breakdowns of systemic significance in the last 25 years—on the average of one every five years. Warning enough that something rather basic is amiss. . . .
>
> It is hard to argue that the new system has brought exceptional benefits to the economy generally. Economic growth and productivity in the last 25 years has been comparable to that of the 1950s and '60s but in the earlier years the prosperity was more widely shared. . . .

Simply stated, the bright new financial system—for all its talented participants, for all its rich rewards—has failed the test of the market place. . . .

Financial crises typically emerge after a self-reinforcing process of market exuberance marked by too much lending and too much borrowing, which in turn develop in response to underlying economic imbalances. . . . [T]he United States as a whole [has become] addicted to spending and consuming beyond its capacity to produce. The result has been a practical disappearance of personal savings, rapidly rising imports, and a huge deficit in trade. . . .

But in the end . . . no financial legerdemain could long sustain the unsustainable. A breaking point appears. . . . The excesses of the sub-prime mortgage were exposed, doubts about financial values spread, and adjustments— painful but necessary adjustments—are forced on the economy. . . .

[And he concluded:]

Let's not lose sight of the silver lining—what can be the positive outcome of all the turbulence. The excesses of the market are surely being penalized in terms of huge losses of money and prestige. The transient pleasures of extreme leveraging have been exposed. By force of circumstances, the nation's spending and consumption are being brought in line with our capacity to produce. The need for regulatory reform is broadly recognized.

At the end of Volcker's address, he was asked by former Blackstone chairman Peter Peterson whether it was true that he had made "a strong statement in support of Barack Obama's presidential candidacy . . . [even though] he has the most liberal voting record in the Senate."

Volcker replied that he hadn't studied Obama's voting record but:

> What I do have is some fairly strong feelings, and I don't like the direction this country has been going in for some time, in many directions. Economics may be part of it, but it is only a small part of the problem in this country. Let me give you a little symptom of a lot that's wrong.
>
> People have been taking surveys of American people every year for years. One of these things where they ask the same question. Do you trust your government to do the right thing most of the time? Not a very tough examination . . . twenty or thirty years ago, the positive response was 70 percent. Now the positive response is 25 to 30 percent. I think that tells you something.[32]

Volcker followed up in November with even more blistering comments at a symposium in London, and spoke his piece yet again at a February 2009 symposium in New York. "We're in the middle of a massive economic crisis," he said. "We're going to hear the reverberations about this for a long time to come." And he scoffed at the notion that clamping down on banks, hedge funds, and other players would stifle "innovation." The only innovation that real people cared about for the previous twenty or thirty years, he said, was "the automatic teller machine."[33]

In January, the Group of Thirty, which Volcker chairs, released an extensively detailed proposal for financial regulatory reform.[34] The objectives of the new framework are to achieve more comprehensive coverage and to focus on systemically important organizations, regardless of their type. There are also a number of detailed recommendations for greater transparency, more consistency across institutional type, better crisis intervention, and improved tools for stability management.

Reading them, it struck me that nearly all of the recommendations, except for a handful that dealt with jurisdictional issues, could be implemented without legislation. When I asked Volcker, he agreed that was probably true. And that's what makes them vintage Volcker. They are deeply informed but marked by practicality, humility, common sense, and a lack of dogma. That's who Volcker is, and we should treasure him for it.

ECONOMICS, MARKETS, AND REALITY

I n the Introduction, I cited the gross misestimations of the 2008 economy by the brightest lights of the economic forecasting profession. My impression has long been that macroeconomic forecasts are nearly useless. As a check, I pulled a decade's economic forecasts from the White House's Council of Economic Advisers. The Council is staffed by top-flight, often Nobel-quality economists, and while their forecasts can have a political tinge, they rarely stray far from the professional consensus. I started with the 1997 report, released early in the year, when the dot-com boom was well underway. The Council thought the economy's maximum sustainable real growth rate was 2.5 percent, and expected 1997 growth of only 2 percent. The actual outcome, however, was a stunning 4.5 percent. In their next report, in early 1998, the Council duly registered their astonishment at such a splendid 1997, but stuck with the expectation of slow growth, predicting a reversion to 2 percent for the new year. But the 1998 outcome, yet again, was more than twice as high as their forecast. They cautiously raised their forecast for 1999, but still seriously erred on the downside. By 2000, finally, they acknowledged a fundamental shift in national productivity, and sharply raised both their near- and medium-term outlooks—just in time for the dot-com bust and the 2001–2002 recession.[1]

The Council's record during the Bush years was no better. They seriously overforecasted growth in 2002 and 2003, and once the economy was in full recovery mode in 2004, confidently expected that high growth had settled in for the long term. The 2008 report expected slower but positive growth in the first half of the year, as investment shifted away from housing, but foresaw a nice recovery in the second half, and a decent year overall. Their outlook for 2009 and 2010 was for solid 3 percent real growth with low inflation and good employment numbers.

In other words, they hadn't a clue. Nor did Fed chairman Ben Bernanke, a fine economist, in February 2007, when he described to a congressional panel what the *New York Times* called a "Goldilocks" economy—neither too hot nor too cold. The weakness in housing, he told them, had stabilized and would not spill over into the rest of the economy. And Bernanke sits at the intersection of as much economic and financial data as anywhere in the world.

In this last chapter, I'd like to push at the question of why Buffett, Soros, and Volcker could all see the crisis coming from far down the road, when the professional forecasters so consistently got it wrong. And the answer, I think, is wrapped up with the state of economics itself.

Understanding what's wrong with economics wouldn't be so important if we treated economists like weathermen or stock gurus. If a weatherman says it's going to rain today, you bring an umbrella, but most of us ignore forecasts that look more than a few days ahead. We watch the antics of a Jim Cramer for the entertainment value, but few serious investors tune in for real advice.

But the economics profession is taken very seriously. Companies build their spending and investment plans around their economists' forecasts, and the government looks to the profession for guidance on an ever-broadening range of public policy questions. Economists will play a major role in setting the Obama administration's health-care agenda, and they are establishing the terms of debate for the economic stimulus program and the financial bailouts.

What I should like to argue here is not so much the deficiencies of economists, but the importance of recognizing the limits of the profession, and its dangers. Within recent memory, the two dominant schools of macroeconomics, broadly defined—Keynesianism and the Chicago School—have each midwifed public policies with devastating economic consequences. The Great Inflation of the 1970s discredited the 1960s brand of neo-Keynesian economic management. And when the Chicago School got its turn, it pushed flamboyant financial engineering and antiregulatory zealotry to the point of nearly destroying the western financial system.

What manner of teaching is this that can wreak such havoc?

THE "SCIENCE" OF ECONOMICS

Modern mathematical economics was a product of the late nineteenth and early twentieth centuries. It was a time when the recent triumphs of physics seemed to hold the promise of bringing a broad swathe of human activity under the control of "science." Karl Pearson, an older colleague of John Maynard Keynes at Cambridge (and a virulent eugenicist), was a seminal figure who proclaimed that, "[T]he field of science is unlimited . . . every group of natural phenomena, every phase of social life, every stage of past or present development is material for science"—because *"The unity of all science consists alone in its method, not in its material"* (Pearson's italics).[2]

Of all the social sciences, economics came closest to mirroring physics. In David Ricardo's idealized corn auction, correct prices arose from the statistical interaction of countless atomized market participants obeying the simple canons of rational self-interest. It looked just like James Clerk Maxwell's gases: The intricate, and random, dance of countless freely colliding molecules was choreographed by a few simple, immutable laws. In Alfred Marshall's *Principles of Economics*, the basic sourcebook of economics for most of the pre-Depression period, he wrote that the differential calculus—the mathematics of smooth, continuous curves that underlies Newton's laws—was the "universal form," even for fields like sociology and biology, and especially for economics.[3]

Not everyone accepted that argument. Some well-known economists pointed out that, in fact, prices often didn't follow the curves in the models—they could be "sticky" and they moved in jumps, not in the continuous, infinitesimal increments of Newton's falling apple. The American professoriate, however, signed on with enthusiasm, even in fields well beyond economics. John Dewey dreamed of a day when schools could be run "on a psychological basis as great factories are run on the basis of chemical and physical science."[4]

Although Keynes was a fine mathematician, he was among the few consistent skeptics of the scientific pretensions of economics:

> Mathematical Psychics [i.e., its application to social and economic studies] has not, as a science or study, fulfilled its early promise. . . . The atomic hypothesis which has worked so splendidly in physics breaks down in psychics. We are faced at every turn with the problems of organic unity, of discreteness, of discontinuity—the whole is not equal to the

sum of the parts, comparisons of quantity fail us, small changes produce large effects, the assumptions of a uniform and homogeneous continuum are not satisfied.[5]

Keynes's biographer, Robert Skidelsky, suggests that Keynes hearkened back to an older, pre-mathematical brand of "political economy," like that of Mill and Hume, that understood society and its commercial and exchange systems as an organism, rich in assumptions and practices that could not be captured in models. And he understood that while the basic equations of physics do not change, those of economics can sometimes turn to quicksilver. Keynes made his famous comment that "in the long run, we are all dead" in the course of arguing against the value of longer-run economic forecasts. The variability of the basic relations of economics, he thought, were such as to make extended projections highly dubious. And he was extremely skeptical of demanding heroic sacrifice in the present for the sake of distant benefits promised by economists.[6]

Nor did Keynes trust large mathematical models. In 1938, he engaged in a debate with Jan Tinbergen, a Dutch mathematician who had built a model of the Netherlands trade flows, and who later built the first comprehensive, national, macroeconomic model, initially for the Netherlands. Keynes was harsh:

> Is it claimed that there is a likelihood that the equations will work approximately *next* time? . . . One can always cook a formula to fit moderately well a limited range of past facts. But what does this prove? What place is left for expectations

and the state of confidence relating to the future? What place is allowed for non-numerical factors, such as inventions, politics, labour troubles, wars, earthquakes, financial crises?[7]

Keynes's most famous work, *The General Theory of Employment, Interest, and Money*, has a minimum of mathematical apparatus. It became widely accepted in academia, however, after John Hicks in Great Britain and Alvin Hansen in the United States developed a mathematized model of the book's main argument. Neoclassical economics assumed that wages, output, and demand were all self-balancing, with temporary maladjustments corrected by the interest rate. Keynes's departure was to show that an economy could reach multiple points of stable equilibria with lower than optimum demand and employment. Temporary government stimulation of demand, therefore, was a potential way out of a depression. Hick's work had put Keynes's book into the format best designed to proliferate through academia. Still Keynes reacted coolly to it, and had little to do with the very rapid extensions of his work that immediately ensued.

The widening availability of powerful computers after World War II pushed the "neo-Keynesian" macroeconomic model-building enterprise into hyperdrive. American academics, especially, forged a rigidly mechanistic vision of the economic apparatus: Pull this lever and investment rises, turn this flywheel and consumption goes up—all the pieces clicking smoothly into place like stainless-steel tumblers. The 1960 election, and John Kennedy's Harvard connections, brought a raft of economists to the White House brimming with confidence in their new policy tools. It was the administration's faith in a *deus in machina* that prompted Kennedy's wildly unprescient declaration in 1962 that there were no ideological issues left to solve; the country faced only "technical problems . . . administrative problems."[8]

The eclipse of neo-Keynesianism amid the inflationary fiasco of the 1970s led to a recovery of the old neoclassical economics associated with the Chicago School, and a burst of new theorizing under the rubric of the "New Classicals." There was also a close linkage between the New Classicals and the "efficient markets" financial theorists at Chicago's Graduate School of Business. The business school was home to Eugene Fama, Merton Miller, and Myron Scholes, among others, who did much of the basic work on modern portfolio theory and the mathematics of derivatives. By the 2000s, like-thinking academics had taken over most American schools of finance and economics, and all the Wall Street firms.

But as the new theories swept the field, the objections raised in the early twentieth century still held. Financial markets, at least in times of stress, did *not* follow the smooth curves of the models.

The 1987 stock market crash offers a nice example. Amid a general sense that markets were rising frothily, academics from Stanford developed "portfolio insurance." A portfolio manager picked a desired floor price for his portfolio, and if prices started to fall toward the floor, computers sold stock futures in the Chicago markets. If the portfolio value fell past the floor, the gains on the futures would offset the losses on the shares. Markets grew bullishly—possibly because so many investors had bought insurance—but there finally came a time when markets weakened to a point where the computer "sell" algorithms kicked in vigorously. But the buyers on the other side did not happen to be computers, coolly calculating mathematically consistent prices. There were only humans, who like most human traders faced with a tsunami of sales, panicked and started selling too. Instead of a smooth, continuous, differentiable price curve, there were long, long moments when there were no prices at all. Black Monday's 23 percent market drop is the largest one-day market drop in history.

In the recent credit debacle, one can make a case that financial modeling practices actually helped *cause* the extremes of leverage that have imploded into the financial rubble around us.

Allow me for a moment to be arcane. The conception of markets at the root of most New Classical macroeconomic models is the so-called "Arrow-Debreu economy." It is the kind of frictionless, perfectly clearing economy that Chicago School economists dream about. But its special feature is that markets are "complete"—any asset or risk position can be seamlessly converted into a "contingent claim"—i.e., a financial derivative. The intuitive idea is that if there are properly priced derivatives covering every kind of risk, all risks will migrate to those most desirous and capable of holding them. The whole system therefore becomes more stable and resilient. The conservative economists at the Federal Reserve bought that reasoning—they actually believed that the explosion of financial derivatives in the 2000s *decreased* risk!* Alan Greenspan said as much many times. And that belief allowed them to ignore the vast

---

* For a detailed statement right on point, see Governor Kevin Warsh, "Financial Intermediation and Complete Markets," Speech at the European Economics and Financial Centre, London, England, June 5, 2007. Note the date: It was about two weeks before the collapse of Bear Stearns mortgage-backed hedge funds—the first sliding pebble in the financial avalanche to come. Warsh, of course, tossed in the appropriate cautions about sufficient liquidity, etc., but the overall tone was that a new day had arrived, and his description of "complete markets" is right out of the New Classical casebook.

buildup of leverage and the proliferation of products that nobody understood.[9]

At bottom, the credit crash is about unbridled greed, chicanery, and outright fraud. It's easy to find many examples. But we've always known that the opportunity to make great wealth will cause even usually decent people to trample conventional notions of honor and ethics. The tougher question is how could the rapacity grow to such a scale without very smart people, like Ben Bernanke, noticing? The answer seems to be that they were looking at the world through a very special set of lenses. Practical people, like Buffett, Soros, and Volcker, and many, many others, could see the very dangerous waters ahead as early as 2003 and 2004, and often well before. But through the magic glasses, with lenses from the dominant schools of academic economics and finance, markets appeared to have attained their heaven, and all was for the best, in the best of all possible worlds.[10]

A SHORT LOOK BACK

It's worth reflecting briefly on how much has gone wrong and how fast it happened. The unique feature of the current crisis is that it is a *balance-sheet* crisis, a credit overshoot, originating within the financial sector. That's one of the reasons it's so nasty. Credit is the air that markets breathe. Toxic credit infects all asset classes, and the American market presence is so big that the infection has spread throughout the world. And the economics profession failed to see it coming, even as the economy grew wildly out of balance.

There was much evidence of things gone awry. Corporate profits grew very strongly in the 2000s. From 1960 through 2007, after-tax corporate profits averaged 6.5 percent of national income. In the four years from 2004 through 2007, the average was 10.8 percent, shooting up to 11.8 percent in 2006 and 2007. But even as profits grew strongly, the rate of corporate investment fell, so free corporate cash flows grew mightily. Conveniently, Congress changed the tax code to encourage cash distribution to shareholders. The companies that make up the S&P 500, from the fourth quarter of 2004 through yearend 2007, made $2.1 trillion in net earnings. They gave all of it back to shareholders in the form of dividends or stock buybacks. Shareholder distributions were about a third larger than capital investment.

Those huge streams of free cash went mostly to institutions and wealthy investors, and were invested primarily in financial instruments. The powerful surge of money into stock and bond markets raised asset prices and drove a steep drop in yields. Falling yields encourage risky behavior like the huge buildup of leveraged trading assets at the biggest banks, and the preference for the higher yields available in consumer debt. The Federal Reserve did nothing to stop the asset boom; indeed, by keeping interest rates inordinately low for an extended period, it greatly encouraged it. The financial sector quickly became the primary driver of the economy, accounting for 40 percent of all corporate profits by 2007.

Disquietingly, something similar happened in the 1920s. Corporate cash flows grew much faster than investment or wages and the excess flowed into financial instruments. There was a burst of inventive consumer lending, both through residential mortgages and installment purchase debt, including some of the same instruments, like interest-only mortgages, that got banks like Countrywide in such trouble. And when banks got worried about their shaky loans, they bundled them up—or "securitized" them—into highly leveraged "investment trusts" that they floated on the stock market. It has a familiar ring.

In our own day, the flood of finance pushed consumer spending to 72 percent of GDP, the highest rate ever, anywhere, while personal savings rates dropped to virtually zero. Very quickly, Americans became grossly overinvested in items that Wall Street was good at financing—bigger houses, SUVs, electronic toys from Asia. Secondary booms duly followed—in new shopping malls; in the shiny new office buildings and the luxury hotels and restaurants that bankers like; and in highly leveraged buyouts of companies riding the same waves, such as hotel chains, retailers, casinos, furniture stores, and home builders. And when there were no good assets to lend against and a dearth of creditworthy borrowers, the financial sector just kept on lending, inventing "ninja" mortgages ("no income, no job or assets"), "no-covenant" company takeover loans (if you can't pay, the lender can't make you), and other corruptions. In the 2000s, Americans spent 105 percent of what they produced, with most of the overrun on the household accounts.

In other words, the economy was completely out of whack. Why couldn't economists see it? Well they did, of course, but since their models assumed that markets are always right, they constructed new theories to explain why markets were behaving the way they were.

A favorite was the "Global Savings Glut," announced with some fanfare by none other than Ben Bernanke in 2005.[11] The idea was that the soaring American international debt and trade deficits were caused by "excess global savings," especially in emerging markets like China. It's not true. At best, global savings were flat in the 2000s. Their *locus* shifted, as the United States ran down its savings to buy consumer goods and oil. It was the American credit binge that was the channel for building emerging market surpluses, lubricated by the near-total deregulation of mortgage and credit card borrowing. (From 2000 through 2007, Americans withdrew $4.2 trillion in mortgage equity from their homes; it was equivalent to 6.1 percent of gross disposable personal income over that period. During that same time, the American goods and services trade deficit was $4.5 trillion. Not a coincidence.)

Without the benefit of modern statistics, and with nary a macro-economic model to lean on, a Nicholas Biddle, a Walter Bagehot, or any other avatar of nineteenth-century central banking would have known what to do when their economy foamed up the way ours did. Tuck up interest rates, slow things down, don't let the trade balance get so far into the hole, rein in government borrowing. It's just common sense.

But America's regulators took no such action. Certainly, putting the brakes on the growing asset bubble would have slowed growth and quite likely caused a recession—but Greenspan had been de-ified for avoiding recessions. And Wall Street would have screamed bloody murder. So they let it rip. And once the cycle locked in, it became self-amplifying as countries like China developed a huge stake in keeping it going. But the fundamental causality ran from America to the world, not the other way round. Theories like the "Global Savings Glut" were a species of panglossian rationalization: Everything was being driven by larger market forces, beyond the control of regulators. But not to worry, it was all part of the benign process by which efficient markets work a smooth rebalancing. In reality the theories were just craven self-exoneration—academic cover for why the authorities stood aside and let Wall Street blow up the world.

Economists do a great deal of useful work—tracking trade flows, for instance, or trying to trace the effects of currency revaluations. But the field is far too immature to encompass the operations of a whole economy, or as the record shows, even make accurate forecasts of gross tendencies. (And if the microvariables of an economy constantly change relations with each other, as Keynes suspected, economics will never be reliably predictive.)

Economics is not a science, like physics. Its methods are primarily analogical and metaphorical. Its data are gross and error-prone, and its models of economic interactions bear only a distant relationship to those in the real world. The theoretical apparatus of economics—its "laws"—are mostly imaginative constructs that can rarely be confirmed with any precision. Their content and structure, moreover, are as often developed from ideological premises as from observation. That's one of the reasons that highly qualified economists can always be found on almost any side of a question—rather like eighteenth-century physicians sniffing a patient's urine and arguing whether the black or the yellow bile is the culprit.

THE DEEPER FLAW

A characteristic of modern economics and finance, especially of the neoclassical or New Classical variety, is the narrowness of its vision. Bruce Scott is a professor at Harvard Business School, and something of a pariah among his colleagues because he insists on teaching capitalism as something more than just business and financial markets. He insists it is a system of governance. It typically has a three-tiered structure, and business schools teach only one of them. He likes to compare the three-tiered structure of American capitalism to that of the National Football League.[12]

The three-tiered structure of the NFL includes a political/governance tier, the league office; an institutional tier, or the teams; and the game itself. The league office establishes the rules of the game, admits qualified teams, and defines allowable technologies and procedures (no helmet-to-helmet hits). At the moment, NFL governors have strong socialistic tendencies, setting salary caps and legislating inter-team revenue sharing. The institutional layer of the NFL (the teams) has substantial legislative power, voting on rule changes or on the admission of new teams. It also supplies stadiums and other physical infrastructure so the games can take place. The games themselves are the competitive arena, although there are elaborate regulations to ensure that the games are consistently played and fairly decided.

The parallels to a capitalist system of governance are obvious. The political authority—the executive, the legislature(s), the courts, and regulatory bodies—establish and enforce the rules of the game and define permissible technologies and qualifications for players. The institutional layer includes stock exchanges, wire transfer systems, and much more, that forms the basic infrastructure for capitalist transactions. And the players are the companies, the traders, the entrepreneurs.

Scott points out that each layer is entrepreneurial, working to expand its scope and freedom of action. In the NFL, defensive ends complain about the elaborate protections for quarterbacks, while the teams with the best wide receivers lobby for tighter rules against hand-checking. The capitalist masters of the universe want fewer restrictions on trading, on leverage, on antitrust restrictions. The infrastructure and political layers lobby to bring hedge funds within the regulatory ambit. The hedge funds counter-argue, in effect, that you'll sell fewer tickets and bring in less revenue.

Scott makes the important point, however, that the political tier has deeper purposes. Capitalism, viewed as a governance system, has a history—in the West, a history of hundreds of years of reining in the looting free-for-alls that only warlords could win. So the rules evolved, to greater or lesser degrees, to curb the appetites of the quick, the deadly, and the unprincipled.* To protect against winner-take-all outcomes. To prevent individual risk-taking with potential systemic consequences. To ensure that even losers don't starve. None of those broader purposes is captured by our currently dominant economic and financial models. The Arrow-Debreu style of economy needs no government whatsoever; it would just get in the way. To stay with the NFL analogy, over the past decade, capitalism turned the game over to a player free-for-all, and discovered what a bloody, ugly scene that can be.

What is striking about Scott's paradigm is that most people— I've tried it out on a number—find it strikingly original, and after thinking about it a bit, utterly obvious. Its apparent originality, I suspect, is because it's something of a throwback. There was a time when people talked and thought about the purposes of government, or of a capitalist system. It was a topic that greatly engaged Keynes, for instance, but it has been of little interest for the past quarter century or longer.

Which brings us back to Soros, Buffett, and Volcker. All of them think in organic terms. Volcker's career has spanned all three layers, but primarily the governing and infrastructure layers. Soros's investing style, as we have seen, is acutely attuned to what is going

---

* The *Wall Street Journal* had the grace and consistency to mock the wealthy erstwhile antiregulatory stalwarts bewailing the SEC's failure to protect them from Bernie Madoff.

on in a society, not just its markets. Buffett talks about the "Ovarian Lottery." "The people who say, 'I did it all myself' and think of themselves as Horatio Alger—believe me, they'd [pay a lot more] to be in the United States than in Bangladesh. That's the Ovarian Lottery."[13]

One can imagine that their broader view is part of the reason why, for a half century, they have navigated multiple markets in multiple stages of crisis and triumph with great success. All three are wise, all three are humble about what they don't know, none of them carries around a definitive "model" of the world. None would ever insist that "only money" or "only demand" is the driving force of the economic universe. They navigate, instead, by relying on their great experience, a sense of history, and their common sense.

The current global economic debacle has discredited almost all the captains of the finance industry, the regulators of most nations, and the gurus in academia. But the Sages stand taller than ever. There is a lesson there, and one hopes the world will learn it.

ACKNOWLEDGMENTS

This book, to a degree unusual for me, was from start to finish a collaborative project with the publisher. Special thanks to Peter Osnos, Susan Weinberg, Lindsay Jones, and Melissa Raymond. My appreciation to Nick Jahr for his careful fact checking, and to Nancy King for her copy editing. And for their help at important points, Michael Vachon at Soros Funds and Larry Malkin, a long-time Volcker collaborator.

As always, appreciation to my agent, Tim Seldes, who has represented me for more than thirty years, and most of all, to my wife, Beverly, who has tolerated my authorial habits even longer than that.

NOTES

INTRODUCTION

1. *Wall Street Journal,* February 13, 2009. The article was accompanied by a downloadable spreadsheet.

SOROS

1. Soros includes sketches of his childhood in most of his books. In addition, there are two biographies of Soros: Michael T. Kaufman, *Soros: The Life and Times of a Messianic Billionaire* (New York: Vintage, 2003), which was written with Soros's cooperation; and Robert Slater, *Soros: The Life, Times and Trading Secrets of the World's Greatest Investor* (New York: McGraw-Hill, 1997). Soros did not cooperate with Slater's book, but the author spoke to many of Soros's colleagues and friends. The quote in the paragraph is from an interview.

2. The thumbnail of Popper is mine, from Karl R. Popper, *The Open Society and Its Enemies,* 5th ed., 2 vols. (Princeton, NJ: Princeton University Press).

3. *Time* magazine, December 31, 1965.

4. Walter Heller, *New Dimensions of Political Economy* (Cambridge, MA: Harvard University Press, 1966), 66.

5. George Soros, interview with author.

6. George Soros, *The Alchemy of Finance* (Hoboken, NJ: John Wiley & Sons, 2003), 68.

7. Soros, interview with author.

8. Ibid.

9. Ibid.

10. Except as otherwise noted, this section, including the quotations, are from Soros, *Alchemy,* 145–315.

11. For background, Mathias Zurlinden, "The Vulnerability of Pegged Exchange Rates: The British Pound in the ERM," Federal Reserve Bank of St. Louis (September–October 1993).

12. Soros, interview with author.

13. Ibid.

14. Ibid.

15. *Times* (London), October 25, 1992.

16. Kaufman, *Soros*, 141; Soros, interview with author.

17. George Soros with Byron Wien and Krisztina Koenen, *Soros on Soros: Staying Ahead of the Curve* (Hoboken, NJ: John Wiley & Sons, 1995).

18. Quoted in Kaufman, *Soros*, 140.

19. George Soros, *Open Society: Reforming Global Capitalism* (New York: PublicAffairs, 2000), 233.

20. Druckenmiller quotations taken from Kaufman, *Soros*, 141–144.

21. Soros, *Open Society*, pp., 215–218.

22. Soros, interview with author.

23. *New York Times*, April 16, 2008, and March 25, 2009.

24. Quoted in Kaufman, *Soros*, 165.

25. Soros, *Soros on Soros*, 112–113.

26. Soros tells the story very well in his book *Underwriting Democracy* (New York: Free Press, 1991).

27. Current information from Open Society Institute, Soros Foundations Network Report, 2007 (New York: OSI, 2008); Kaufman, *Soros*, has a good history of the philanthropies.

28. Except as noted, this section is based on interviews and unpublished material furnished by Soros.

29. George Soros, *The New Paradigm for Financial Markets: The Credit Crisis of 2008 and What It Means* (New York: PublicAffairs, 2008), 144.

30. Soros, *Open Society*, 294.

31. Soros, interview with author.

32. Ibid.

BUFFETT

1. Benjamin Graham and David L. Dodd, *Security Analysis*, 1951 ed. (New York: McGraw-Hill, 2005), 389.

2. Ibid., 408.

3. All quotes from and about this event are from Buffett's after-the-fact written version, Warren E. Buffett, "The Superinvestors of Graham-and-Doddsville," *Hermes* (1984); reprint available at http://www4.gsb.columbia.edu/hermes/superinvestors. The table is mine from the data provided in the talk.

4. Biographical detail and investing history follow Alice Schroeder, *The Snowball: Warren Buffett and the Business of Life* (New York: Bantam Books, 2008); Roger Lowenstein, *Buffett: The Making of an American Capitalist* (New York: Random House, 1995); and the Annual Reports of Berkshire Hathaway. The Schroeder book was written with Buffett's complete cooperation. Buffett never spoke to Lowenstein, but he didn't prevent anyone else from speaking with him. Both books are superb and, in researching individual deals, I generally used both. Because Schroeder conducted extensive interviews with Buffett, and accompanied him on important trips, she is the major source for Buffett quotes.

5. Schroeder, *Snowball*, 201.

6. Ibid., 241.

7. Ibid., 265.

8. Ibid., 414.

9. Ibid., 466.

10. Adam Smith, *Supermoney* (New York: Wiley, 2006), 190.

11. Berkshire Hathaway Inc., Chairman's Letter to Shareholders, 1984.

12. Schroeder, *Snowball*, 602.

13. Ibid., 198.

14. House Committee on Banking and Financial Services, October 1, 1998.

15. Schroeder, *Snowball*, 659.

16. Berkshire Hathaway Inc., Chairman's Letter to Shareholders, 2007.

17. PBS Nightly Business Report, January 22, 2009; transcript available at http://www.pbs.org/nbr/site/onair/transcripts/090122t/.

VOLCKER

1. I interviewed Volcker in 2007 for *The Trillion Dollar Meltdown*, and again while I was preparing this book. For various reasons, he asked that he not be directly quoted from the second interview.

2. Paul A. Volcker and Toyoo Gyohten, *Changing Fortunes: The World's Money and the Threat to American Leadership* (New York: Times Books, 1992), 47.

3. All economic data in this chapter are from official government sources.

4. Robert L. Bartley, *The Seven Fat Years and How to Do it Again* (New York: Free Press, 1992), 27.

5. Volcker, *Changing Fortunes*, 79–80.

6. William Greider, *Secrets of the Temple: How the Federal Reserve Runs the Country* (New York: Simon & Schuster, 1987), 433.

7. Ibid., 66.

8. Ibid., 47.

9. Michael J. Boskin, *Reagan and the Economy: The Successes, Failures and Unfinished Agenda* (Panama City, Panama: International Center for Economic Growth, 1988), 88.

10. Transcript of Federal Open Market Committee meeting, October 5, 1982, 19.

11. Paul Volcker, interview with author.

12. Transcript of Federal Open Market Committee meeting, September 18, 1979, 34.

13. Transcript of Federal Open Market Committee meeting, February 2–3, 1981, 35. (Greider's footnote quote in *Secrets*, 392.)

14. Quotes in this and two preceding paragraphs taken from transcript of Federal Open Market Committee meeting, October 6, 1979, 6, 8, 9, 17.

15. *New York Times*, October 14, 1979.

16. Transcript of Federal Open Market Committee meeting, January 8–9, 1980, 2

17. Transcript of Federal Open Market Committee meeting, May 20, 1980, 10, 23–24.

18. Transcript of Federal Open Market Committee meeting, February 2–3, 1981, 77.

19. Bartley, *Seven Fat Years*, 114–115.

20. Transcript of Federal Open Market Committee meeting, March 29, 1982, 24.

21. Greider, *Secrets*, 465.

22. Leonard Silk, "Economic Scene: The New Pragmatism," *New York Times*, July 28, 1982.

23. Except as indicated, the account of the LDC crisis follows Federal Deposit Insurance Corporation, *History of the Eighties: Lessons for the Future*, vol. 1, *The LDC Debt Crisis* (Washington, DC: USGPO, 1997), 192–210.

24. Transcript of Federal Open Market Committee meeting, October 5, 1982, 21.

25. Volcker quotes in this and the preceding paragraph from ibid., 19–21.

26. Greider, *Secrets*, 194.

27. Joseph B. Treaster, *Paul Volcker: The Making of a Financial Legend* (Hoboken, NJ: Wiley, 2004), 181.

28. *New York Times*, June 11, 1997, and January 23, 2000.

29. The data in the preceding paragraphs are drawn from the reports of the inquiry committee. They are available at http://www.iic-offp.org/story27oct05.htm.

30. Ben Heineman, interview with author. The final report is available at http://siteresources.worldbank.org/NEWS/Resources/Volcker_Report_Sept._12,_for_website_FINAL.pdf.

31. *New York Times*, October 24, 2008.

32. Transcript of Volcker's speech to Economic Club of New York, April 8, 2008. Available at http://econclubny.org/files/Transcript_Volcker_April_2008.pdf.

33. *New York Times*, February 6, 2009.

34. *Financial Reform: A Blueprint for Financial Stability* (Washington, DC: Group of Thirty, 2009). Available at http://www.group30.org/pubs/pub_1460.htm.

ECONOMICS, MARKETS, AND REALITY

1. The forecast data from the *Annual Reports* of the Council of Economic Advisers; the actual outcomes are from the Commerce Department.

2. Karl Pearson, *The Grammar of Science* (New York: Cosimo Classics, 2007), 12. *Grammar* was first published in 1892.

3. I used an open-source version of Marshall's *Principles* at http://www.econlib.org/library/Marshall/marP27.html. The quotation is from the mathematical Appendix, which is not paginated.

4. Dorothy Ross, *The Origins of American Social Science* (New York: Cambridge University Press, 1991), 219–256. Quotations taken from p. 253.

5. Robert Skidelsky, *John Maynard Keynes, 1883–1946: Economist, Philosopher, Statesman* (New York: Penguin Books, 2003), 460.

6. Ibid., 392.

7. Ibid., 549–550.

8. Henry J. Aaron, *Politics and the Professors: The Great Society in Perspective* (Washington, DC: Brookings, 1978), 167.

9. David Colander, et. al., "The Financial Crisis and the Systemic Failure of Economics" (not yet published but available at http://www.debtdeflation.com/blogs/wp-content/uploads/papers/Dahlem_Report_EconCrisis021809.pdf)

10. See, for example, "Risk and Uncertainty in Monetary Policy," Remarks by Chairman Alan Greenspan, Federal Reserve Board, January 3, 2004; and "The Great Moderation," Remarks by Governor Ben S. Bernanke, Federal Reserve Board, February 20, 2004.

11. Ben S. Bernanke, "The Global Savings Glut and the U.S. Current Account Deficit," Federal Reserve, March 10, 2005.

12. Scott is currently seeing a major book into press, but he has shared parts of it with me.

13. Schroeder, *Snowball*, 643–644.

INDEX

Andrew Popper

In addition to the recent *New York Times* bestseller *The Trillion Dollar Meltdown*, Charles R. Morris has written eleven books, including *The Tycoons*, a *Barron's* Best Book of 2005. A lawyer and former banker, Mr. Morris's articles and reviews have appeared in many publications including *The Atlantic Monthly*, the *New York Times*, and the *Wall Street Journal*.

PublicAffairs is a publishing house founded in 1997. It is a tribute to the standards, values, and flair of three persons who have served as mentors to countless reporters, writers, editors, and book people of all kinds, including me.

I. F. Stone, proprietor of *I. F. Stone's Weekly*, combined a commitment to the First Amendment with entrepreneurial zeal and reporting skill and became one of the great independent journalists in American history. At the age of eighty, Izzy published *The Trial of Socrates*, which was a national bestseller. He wrote the book after he taught himself ancient Greek.

Benjamin C. Bradlee was for nearly thirty years the charismatic editorial leader of *The Washington Post*. It was Ben who gave the *Post* the range and courage to pursue such historic issues as Watergate. He supported his reporters with a tenacity that made them fearless and it is no accident that so many became authors of influential, best-selling books.

Robert L. Bernstein, the chief executive of Random House for more than a quarter century, guided one of the nation's premier publishing houses. Bob was personally responsible for many books of political dissent and argument that challenged tyranny around the globe. He is also the founder and longtime chair of Human Rights Watch, one of the most respected human rights organizations in the world.

. . .

For fifty years, the banner of Public Affairs Press was carried by its owner Morris B. Schnapper, who published Gandhi, Nasser, Toynbee, Truman, and about 1,500 other authors. In 1983, Schnapper was described by *The Washington Post* as "a redoubtable gadfly." His legacy will endure in the books to come.

Peter Osnos, *Founder and Editor-at-Large*